D0072279

Dramatherapy with Families, Groups and Individuals

Waiting in the Wings

Books of related interest

Art Therapy and Dramatherapy: Their Relation and Practice
Sue Jennings and Ase Minde
ISBN 1 85302 027 3

Storymaking in Education and Therapy
Alida Gersie and Nancy King
ISBN 1 85302 519 4

Storymaking in Bereavement
Alida Gersie
ISBN 1 85302 065 6

Time, Energy and the Psychology of Healing
Helen Graham
ISBN 1 85302 066 4

Drama and Healing: The Roots of Dramatherapy
Roger Grainger
ISBN 1 85302 048 6

Art Therapy in Practice
Edited by Marian Liebmann
ISBN 1 85302 057 5

Christian Symbols, Ancient Roots
Sue Jennings and Elizabeth Rees
ISBN 1 85302 046 X

Structuring the Therapeutic Process:
Compromise with Chaos: The Therapist's Response
to the Individual and the Group
Murray Cox
ISBN 1 85302 028 1

Coding the Therapeutic Process:
Emblems of Encounter: A Manual for
Counsellors and Therapists
Murray Cox
ISBN 1 85302 029 X

Dramatherapy with Families, Groups and Individuals

Waiting in the Wings

Sue Jennings

Jessica Kingsley Publishers
London

Illustrations based on original drawings by Audrey Hillyar

First published in 1990 by
Jessica Kingsley Publishers Ltd
118 Pentonville Road
London N1 9JN

British Library Cataloguing in Publication Data
is available

ISBN 1 85302 014 1

Printed and bound in Great Britain by
Biddles Ltd, Guildford and King's Lynn

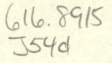
dedicated to the memory
of the late
Harry Andrews
friend for 35 years
and patron of my endeavours

Acknowledgements

Writing books is such an anti-social activity that this time I would like to thank all my friends who have put up with my cloisterdom and looked kindly on my occasional mole-like emergence into the ordinary world.

Colleagues, clients and patients have been always generous with their time, scenes and images.

Andy, Ros and Hal, my children, continue to give me nurture, stimulus and provocation, both on-stage and off.

Murray Cox, Hugh and Jean Dickinson, Mother Lucia, Clare Higgins, Audrey Hillyar, Jessica Kingsley, Robert Silman and Aasmund Vik provide me with the inspiration and support that a body and soul could wish for. I thank them.

I wish to express my appreciation to the following authors and publishers for permission to quote the following extracts:

Bely, A., 1985, *The Jaws of the Night*, in *Doubles, Demons and Dreamers: an international collection of symbolist drama* (ed. Gerould), Performing Arts Journal Publications, New York, p 177

Brooke, P., 1972, *The Empty Space*, Penguin, London, p 11

Miles, B., and Trewin, J. C., 1981, *Curtain Calls*, Lutterworth Press, Guildford, p 11

Pirandello, L., 1979, *Six Characters In Search of an Author* in *Three Plays* (trans. Rietty/Mitchell/Londstrom), Methuen, London, Act III.i.

Schaffer, P., 1976, *Five Finger Exercise*, Penguin, Harmondsworth, Act I.ii.

The identifying factors of all therapeutic material have been changed to preserve anonymity.

Sue Jennings

Contents

Introduction

'Must I say something?
Can it be wrong tomorrow?
Will you let me be wrong?
Or can I change my mind?'

Sarah aged 15 in an improvisation

Dramatherapy is an art form which has emerged as a clinical and educational practice during the past 30 years; a process in which I have been deeply involved. The roots of my own dramatherapy experience began at the age of 17, when I was an auxiliary nurse in a psychiatric hospital during academic breaks from drama college. However, it is clear to me that we are not talking about a new therapeutic and art form; ancient civilisations all over the world have used drama and theatre as part of ritual and a healing process, for thousands, if not millions of years.

However, it is new in a western culture to recognise the therapeutic potential of the arts within medical practice. One of the dilemmas of the arts therapist is to find a balanced relationship between traditional medical practice on the one hand, and the ancient folk art culture on the other. The former is of this century and is considered scientific and measurable; the other is archaic, existing before written history, artistic and immeasurable. Yet both have their mysteries, costumes, language and procedures. They share the use of theatres, masks and rituals, sacred spaces and long initiation. Even so, it is only now that they are in discourse. It is very recent that the relationship between drama and medicine begins.

Early dramatherapists sought to compensate for this by working in a medical model; in fact one practitioner was threatened with dismissal if she did not practice in this way. It has taken work over the last 25 years for dramatherapists to reach the point where they can articulate their philosophy without needing to use other disciplines to authenticate it.

Dramatherapy is based on our knowledge and understanding of drama, theatre and ritual processes. A working understanding of Aristotle, Plato, Stanislavski,

Brecht, Grotowski, Wilshire, Victor Turner Boal and Peter Brook, together with an in-depth knowledge of major plays from ancient Greece, and Shakespeare through to Beckett, Sartre and Pinter, and on to the immediate present with Caryl Churchill and David Hare;[1] a thorough grounding in movement, improvisation, scripts, performance, masks, myth; as actor, director and choreographer. This is the foundation of being a dramatherapist.

Of course, clinical knowledge is necessary (psychiatry, psychology, psychotherapy) to understand the pathology of the people with whom we may work, as well as the nature of human development in its many forms. We need to know about the most recent discoveries about brain function as well as the workings of the unconscious. And dramatherapists can never know enough about symbol, ritual, metaphor and role.[2]

There comes a point when we need to return to the root base - the theatre - yet again, to understand dramatherapy. It is as if there is a spiral of knowledge and experience to which we keep returning, to gain more insight and knowledge; the dramatherapist is always on a journey, both inner and outer.

Dramatherapy is not a medical science or a psychotherapy in the accepted frames of reference. Medical science informs it largely by providing greater understanding of the people with whom we work. Everything that can tell us more about the human condition, whether anatomical, biological, intra-psychic or social, serves to inform us yet more in this still uncharted land.

This book is intended to take people a little further into this land. It cannot be a definitive statement but is intended to bring together some experience and thinking along the way.

I am indebted to the many practitioners and writers from many and varied disciplines that I have encountered in my continued exploration of dramatherapy. Their influence is apparent in my writing.

I have tried to keep jargon and specialist terminology to a minimum but there are some words which may need clarification. I refer several times to the embodiment-projection-role paradigm. This is my way of describing the developmental process of human dramatic growth.

It begins with the senses soon after birth which are experienced through the human body, and exploration and development of *bodily experience* into a sense of self and then a body image of that self. Human beings *project* their experience through media outside themselves. We work with this capacity through sculpting - the use of objects or people to represent the dynamics of a situation. The capacity to play *roles* gradually develops in human beings from the early beginnings in dramatic play.

I refer several times to transference and intra-psychic processes, both terms used in psychotherapy. Transference is the human propensity to transfer feelings that belong to people in our past experience to people we encounter in the present. Psychoanalysts and psychotherapists use it to describe the varied feelings transfered onto the therapist. Intra-psychic processes are those which are within the human psyche. One of the aims of therapy is to influence these processes if they block our healthy functioning.

Many people want to understand the difference between psychodrama and dramatherapy. Psychodrama, developed in the USA by Moreno[3] earlier this century, builds on human beings' capacity to dramatise through the use of role play, role reversal and other psychodramatic methods. Psychodrama is a form of group psychotherapy, which makes use of dramatic techniques and emphasises the importance of catharsis. Dramatherapy shares many methods with psychodrama, but emphasises the art form of drama and theatre as its central focus.

Although this book is about dramatherapy, there are many other therapists who incorporate a dramatherapeutic approach into the way they work. Systemic family therapists make use of sculpting; group psychotherapists use role-play from time to time. There are also some dramatherapists who practice within a particular framework; they may, for example, choose the insight and understanding drawn from the psychology of Jung to underpin their practice.

There are many variations on the theme of dramatherapy, and a continuing struggles to understand the myriad of processes that it contains. This has led to various splits in ideology and practice between different 'schools' of dramatherapy thinking. In recent times there has been a building of bridges between the various orientations[4] and an encouraging increase in dialogue between more and more of the therapeutic professions. I find it very heartening that ways can be found for communication to be maintained - that groups of people can acknowledge difference as well as similarity. No-one has a prior claim to the 'rightness' of a therapeutic approach, and the map is still sufficiently unexplored for us all to have some space.

> 'From you I have plucked a violet that will never fade. You are all covered with violets; God's bees, God's golden bees, are flying after me! I shall bring you a little bouquet, I shall come to you all bright and shining. I am bearing holiness in my hands like a tiny handful of brightness.'
>
> *Bely: The Jaws of Night (the child), p 177*

Sue Jennings
Stratford-upon-Avon

Chapter One

Scene Setting and Shaping

'Is it not monstrous that this player here,
But in a fiction, in a dream of passion,
Could force his soul so to his own conceit
That from her working all his visage wanned,
Tears in his eyes, distraction in his aspect,
A broken voice, and his whole function suiting
With forms to his conceit? And all for nothing.
For Hecuba!
What's Hecuba to him, or he to her,
That he should weep for her?'

Shakespeare: Hamlet. II.ii

Dramatherapy as an art form

Dramatherapy is an art form and as an art form has the potential for healing. It has the potential for allowing people to view and experience the unhelpful stages of their lives and transform them.

Drama, as rehearsal and performance, is intrinsic to human development, as we can first observe in the healthy development of infants, and then in the emergent roles we all play out in life. For many people, understanding stops at this point. Childrens' capacity to play and the public and private roles that we play in life have been observed and documented by psychologists and anthropologists. However, there appears to be a sticking point when we are relating the drama of life to drama and theatre as an art form. Specialists who are not of drama and theatre claim the specialist's knowledge and understanding of peoples' dramatic behaviour.

Hamlet's speech quoted above highlights for us all this struggle to understand the drama; how is it that an actor can cry, be distracted, and broken voiced 'in a fiction, in a dream of passion' when ordinary people 'can say nothing'? Dramatherapy is about creating this 'fiction' in order for people to understand themselves in new ways through dramatic interaction on a therapeutic stage. Through the creation of fiction and the entering of fictive characters we not only understand ourselves better, but are able to communicate things that otherwise we could not.

Many characters in plays express feelings and emotions that we could not express ourselves, often making use of masks to contain the experience. This has always been one of the functions of the theatre. Dramatherapy provides for people a means of being able to participate in this process directly, within the boundaries of a therapeutic group. Furthermore, because time and space can be represented in a condensed form within the theatre, whole life experiences can be contained and understood that are otherwise too enormous for the human brain to take in at once.

In this chapter I look at the relationship between dramatherapy and our everyday dramas and the dramas of the theatre, and the misgivings that people have about drama and dramatherapy. It is important to remember that there are a series of polarities that people try to maintain, such as separating:

— dramatherapy from drama/theatre
— everyday drama from theatre
— ritual from drama
— role play from drama
— theatre from drama

It is curious that we have to say, 'drama and theatre' when a musician says 'music' and an artist says 'art' and a dancer says 'dance'. Of all the art forms, drama/theatre is the one we find hardest to define, give the least credence to and feel most anxious about.

Is it surprising that dramatherapists struggle with their art and craft, when we have struggled for several thousands of years to understand the drama?

These terms that we try and separate - play, drama, ritual, theatre, role-play, performance - are all part of the same process. This process is an intrinsically human propensity to dramatise, enact and re-enact life experiences in different forms, for different audiences at different times in our lives - what I term the essential *re-working* of experience.

Dramatherapy takes this essentially human process and enables people who are stuck on their journey through life to find some kind of freedom. Let us now take this human process and consider the various elements in relation to the whole.

Drama and play

'Stop playing about'; 'it's only play'; 'when you have finished your work, you can go out to play'.

These familiar phrases illustrate our ambivalence about reality and play and the work ethic and play. Even with the advancements in understanding of brain function and human development, it is culturally very hard for people to accept that play is something people *have to do*. Many play specialists have developed theories of play in relation to learning, (conceptual, social, motor, and so on) but all emphasise the crucial importance of play experience. Play starts much earlier than we usually acknowledge. Babies show the capacity to dramatise within months of being born. Let us therefore start at the beginning.

From birth to a year old the baby is involved in a variety of explorations of the senses. It can make sounds and rhythms, it can make marks (albeit with food and faeces), and it can imitate. The infant can do all these things before it walks, and on walking these sensory explorations gain a larger environment in which they can be developed. I term these *pre-play activities* (Jennings 1987) which become developed into play activity from about one year onwards, depending on the familial and cultural environment of the family and the society.

Once the infant is finger painting and playing with toys and objects outside itself, it is moving from the *embodiment* stage of experience to the *projective* stage. Experiences are played out and discovered through media outside the infant, although there are still bodily reactions to the play; for example the feelings associated with making a mess or pouring water. Dramatic play then develops through situational dramatic events from real life, stories and fairy tales. The infant starts to take on the *roles* playing many parts and changing voices. They are able to role-reverse with toys from an early age. The infant has progressed, cumulatively through the stages of *embodiment, projection* and then *role*. If not before, by the age of six, we are very much aware of the well known quotation:

> '............................All the world's a stage,
> And all the men and women merely players.
> They have their exits and their entrances,
> And each man in his time plays many parts.'
>
> *Shakespeare: As You Like It. II. vii*

What is important in understanding the drama is that we grasp the inherent symbolism in dramatic play.

> 'The appearance of symbolism ... is the crucial point in all interpretations of ludic function. Why is it that play becomes symbolic, instead of continuing to be mere sensory motor exercise or intellectual experiment, and why should the enjoyment of movement, or activity for the fun of activity, which constitutes a kind of practical make-believe, be completed at a given moment by imaginative make-believe?'
>
> *Piaget: Play, Dreams and Imitations in Childhood, p 162*

> 'Play is not "ordinary" or "real" life. It is rather a stepping out of "real" life into a temporary sphere of activity with a disposition all of its own. Every child knows perfectly well that he is "only pretending" or that it was "only for fun".'
>
> *Huizinga: Homo Ludens: A Study of the Play Element in Culture, p 8*

Play is a developmental activity through which human beings explore and discover their identity in relation to others through multiple media including their own bodies, projective media and a variety of role-play. Play encourages symbolic thought and action and stimulates the emergence of metaphoric expression. In play we learn to create as well as to set limits; we learn about freedom as well as its boundaries. The human body is the primary means of learning and experiences in play gradually develop in relation to surrounding space. However, play occurs in a symbolic space, a special space set apart that is imbued with significance for the duration of the play activity.

> 'It is 'played out' within certain limits of time and place. It contains its own course and meaning.'
>
> *(ibid, p 9)*

I do not want to elaborate here the many theories of play and development,[1] but I want to draw attention to the importance of play in the ontological development of human beings; although satisfactory play experiences are crucial for the development of gross and fine motor skills, identity, relationships, imagination and conceptual thought, I want to stress the importance of play in relation to what we call the arts. Play itself is the activity that is at the root of artistic expression, particularly drama. How it develops and whether it will move into what we choose to call artistic activity is culturally determined.

Contemporary psychologists have suggested that the two brain hemispheres control complementary areas of activity: there seems to be a dominance in our society of left brain activity (logic, reasoning, words) over right brain activity (intuition, creativity, metaphor). In our culture, education at all levels places greater value on science and technology than on the arts. This suggests that we are increasingly left brain dominated. It is also noticeable that left brain problem solving and computerised play are stimulated earlier and earlier. Thus it is more difficult to acknowledge the crucial role of play activity as contributing to the healthy development of normal human beings. But dramatic play is an in-built, self-regulating activity that enables us to keep a balance between our inner and outer life and our various selves that are able to interact with each other and those around us. You may well agree, in relation to your own life and the children with whom you work, that play is important; perhaps you feel that it should only belong to the world of the child. Let us keep at the back of our minds the development paradigm: embodiment, projection, role - that takes us from pre-play activity to dramatic play, and now move on to consider ourselves as adults.

Drama as adults: the re-working of experience

Try and recall when you last wanted to tell someone about something that happened to you recently; perhaps you had to complain about something, maybe you were involved in an accident or incident. See if you can recall how you told it to someone else. Let us imagine that it was a visit to an out-patients department, where you have been asked to have an X-ray. You are sitting waiting, there are several people in front of you and you start to take notice as someone comes in carrying a child that is looking very ill and pale. There is a flurry of activity. Its mother is weeping and trying to explain to the nurse at the desk what is wrong. She goes away to consult someone else. The junior doctor comes and takes mother and child through to the consulting room. The people left in the waiting room start to speculate on what might be wrong and also how much longer they will have to wait.

Several things start to happen with this scenario. First of all there is a dramatic event that impinges onto us, not only engaging us as an audience but also as participant. We have been affected by what has gone on; we have opinions and thoughts about it. Secondly, we move into a change of role within the scene and also in relation to the other people with us who may be total strangers. People adopt various stances in relation to each other and the event. Maybe someone knows the woman and says, 'Of course last time she brought him here he was only on the support machine just in time'. We listen to her extra knowledge and expand our own perception of the scene. We may be concerned about the outcome and wait to see what happens, or we might be annoyed by the fact that we have had to wait even longer, and we have an important engagement, and so on. Whatever our response, we have become involved in the drama.

The next stage is equally important to the outcome of the drama for us. Usually we tell someone about something that happened to us. Notice how when we do that we, in some small or large way, re-live the event. We create the atmosphere, we give the different parts authentic voices and gestures; we 'set the scene'. We 're-work' the experience for other people and the way we re-work it will depend on the audience. For example, we would tell the story differently to a friend who was a doctor, or our mother, or a friend who had a small baby of the same age as the one taken into hospital. It appears to be an essential part of human function that we re-work various experiences in dramatic form.

When we observe or indulge in gossip,[2] we can see how very clearly defined roles start to emerge in the re-dramatisation. Usually gossip is a re-working of someone else's life experience and not our own. If it is malicious gossip we fill in extra details or invent them. However, we need an audience for the gossip, in the same way as we need an audience for re-working our own personal experiences (Jennings 1988). Above all we need it to be believed, even if the listeners suggest other ways of looking at the material.

Telling the same story

Already we can see how we as adults are involved in the dramatisation of our lives as a way of communication and as a way of dealing with it. The story told many times may not need to be told again. However, when the person is not listened to, or their experience is not affirmed, we may find that they are always telling the same story.

We observe this most frequently in elderly people who tend to get locked into one part of their lives and go on repeating stories about it. How often do the war stories come out to fellow war veterans, or to the next generation? For some of our clients, the repeated story can be more entrenched, as if the person has become stuck at some point of their history and cannot move on.

However, what is important for us to remember is that we do not just *tell* the story, that is, it is not just verbal reportage; we dramatise it, we embody it, project it and enter into role with a number of variations in the drama. We may be accused of 'being too dramatic' or 'treating life as if it was a Greek Tragedy'. We also find that we feel guilty about telling the story; maybe we are being disloyal, maybe we do not have a ready audience, maybe we have been brought up to keep 'ourselves to ourselves'.

Dreaming in dramatic form

There is an optimum amount of re-working that we need to perform in order to allow healthy psychic functioning.

Therefore, one of the functions of dramatherapy is to allow re-working of experience that has not been dealt with; as we observed with dramatic play, the re-working may be in symbolic form, in ritual, in myth, or in the themes from the great dramas of the world which are also our dramas. I shall describe in detail various ways that this re-working takes place in dramatherapeutic application in the following chapters. Before moving on, I want to describe how some of our re-working of life through drama takes place in our dreams.

All of us dream in dramatic form,[3] as though it were a small theatre that is personal to us, playing and re-playing the dramas that, for whatever reason, we need to see. Whatever our theories of dreams, whether we choose to analyse them, write about them, use them as sources of inspiration, or totally dismiss them, nevertheless we dream in dramas.

The Temiar tribe of Malaysia (Jennings 1985, 1987, 1990) believes there is a direct relationship between the private dreams of individuals and the public seances for the group. They believe that dreams reveal, and much of what they reveal is important for the community as a whole, as well as for individuals, whether it is a new song, story or healing method or dance. Dream material will often be used as a basis for the communal seances which are held either to maintain the well being of the community, or to cure sick individuals. Shamans themselves will have become shamans by dreaming of their spirit guides, who will act as their assistants and also as their teachers; role reversal occurs in the Temiar dreams.[4] There is a direct connection between the private dramas of dream and the public dramas of the healing seances; a continuity that 'makes sense' for the participants within their belief system.

For many of us, our private dream dramas and private waking dramas are separated from our public dramas and theatre dramas. It is not that dramatherapy should cause all to be exposed - a stripping of the defence system. It is the carrying through of symbol and metaphor from one to the other, from the private to the public, from the conscious to the unconscious or vice versa that enables change to take place and the healing of splits. Dramatherapists work with dream material, making it possible for the private dramas to be enacted and expanded rather than interpreted.

The first part of this chapter has described how we are all, both as children and adults, engaged in several forms of drama - exploring, enacting, and re-working our experiences through embodying, projecting and role-playing them. It is a very human way of journeying through our lives.

Let us now look at some of the misgivings that people feel about drama, especially when it is used therapeutically.

Critique of drama and therefore dramatherapy

1. Drama is dangerous

I have written elsewhere on the belief that *drama is dangerous*, that it can arouse powerful emotions that get out of control (Jennings 1978, 1987). It is true that drama is a very powerful stimulus that, if negligently applied or provoked, can result in destructive experiences. Plato was very condemnatory of the actor's capacity to enact anti-social feelings.

> 'Then is it really right, to admire when we see him on the stage,
> a man we ourselves be ashamed to resemble? Is it reasonable
> to feel enjoyment and admiration rather than disgust?'
>
> *Plato: The Republic, p 436*

For Plato the creation of images is the lowest level of mental functioning and art is an avoidance of reality. He said that any actor who could act any part well, should be honoured highly and escorted speedily out of the city.

What we need to remember is that the drama is powerful and, properly harnessed, can be a medium for change and understanding. It is the way it is done, not the drama itself that should be heeded. As we saw earlier, when discussing play, a special place, set apart, is necessary for the drama to take place where boundaries of time and activity are established and ground rules understood. With a dramatic structure we are then able to explore within that structure the stories of the human beings involved.

2. Drama is not real and therefore nothing to do with life

People seem very concerned that drama is 'only acting'; 'not real'; 'pretending'; and therefore nothing to do with the realities of life and living. In fact it is suggested that drama encourages peoples' fantasies or could drive them into psychosis.

Earlier in this chapter we saw the same critique applied to play - it is only playing (make believe) - and therefore not true. It is as if the only truth that can be tolerated is a logistic, factual truth backed up by statistics. *Dramatic truth, like poetic truth, is another type of truth*. It is a way of expressing ourselves other than through logical analysis.

So when we enter the drama or the play, or playful drama, or dramatic play, we are not only stepping into another time and space, we are stepping into another reality which has its own truths, its own logic and its own expression. It is fiction.[5]

3. Drama is confusing, especially for people with identity problems

The criticism usually goes something like this - 'drama is about pretending to be other people; it confuses people even more if they do not know who they already are ...'

The very paradox of drama is that we understand more about ourselves because we have played at being other people. This is not a recent idea as George Herbert Mead has pointed out:

> 'In the human group, on the other hand, there is not only this kind of communication but also that in which the person who uses this gesture and so communicates assumes the attitude of the other individual as well as calling it out in the other. He himself is in the role of the other person whom he is so exciting and influencing. It is through taking this role of the other that he is able to come back on himself and so direct his own process of communication. This taking the role of the other, an

expression I have so often used, is not simply of passing importance. It is not something that just happens as an incidental result of the gesture, but it is of importance in the development of co-operative activity. The immediate effect of such role-taking lies in the control which the individual is able to exercise over his own response. The control of the action of the individual in a co-operative process can take place in the conduct of the individual himself if he can take the role of the other.'

G. H. Mead: Mind, Self and Society, p 252

More recently, Grainger (1988, 1989, 1990) has shown that people suffering from thought disorder, become *less* confused when they have been in a dramatherapy group, rather than more confused in their thought. In direct contrast to making people more confused, dramatherapy leads to greater clarity in self-perception as well as enhanced relationships with other people.

Having discussed three criticisms or misgivings that are often expressed about drama and dramatherapy, I want to now further clarify the relationship between dramatherapy and psychodrama. In the Introduction, I referred to the historic emergence of these two forms of therapy that make use of the dramatic mode, and the following is a description of a therapeutic intervention that could have been either psychodramatic or dramatherapeutic.

Dramatherapy and psychodrama: decision on dramatic distancing

Psychodrama method involves patients and clients in the dramatisation of their own material using other members of the group to play roles that occur in their own family or life generally. Peoples' own life material is presented in dramatic form through techniques of role play, empty chair, role reversal and so on. It may be material from the past, present or future. Here people are not dramatically distanced from the material.

Dramatherapy method, although it sometimes uses direct experience, more usually works through the play, myth, scenario, dramatic themes that either exist or can be created by group members. Themes from direct experience connect with the themes of the universal dramas, thereby including in the great story the stories of individuals and the group as a whole. Themes may be from the past, present or future, or may be timeless. In dramatherapy, people are dramatically distanced from their material.

Scheff (1979) and Landy (1986) present extensive theory on distancing mechanisms and catharsis in relation to theatre, psychotherapy and dramatherapy. Their case is a strong one in relation to understanding therapeutic structures in relation to patients' needs - i.e. we must be aware diagnostically of the emotional distance or nearness of the client in relation to the manifesting problem. Thus it is possible for a person to be underdistanced/overdistanced and so on, and the aim of therapy is to find a balance. This influences the therapist in choosing the appropriate therapeutic mode. Landy says:

> 'the more the drama therapist chooses theatrically stylized devices for treatment (i.e. masks, puppets epic theatre techniques) the more he [sic] overdistances the client. In choosing more realistic devices, such as psychodrama and documentary techniques, the therapist will create less distance.'
>
> *Landy: Drama Therapy: Concepts and Practices, p 103*

My own view, following from this statement, is that the dramatic distance in itself usually allows for greater therapeutic movement in terms of both intra-psychic and inter-personal exploration. The dramatic distancing in itself provides a structure for participants that paradoxically brings them closer to themselves.

This is possible both through the dramatic/theatrical structure and the resonance of the dramatic symbols, metaphors and characters. A character is more than a role - a character has a totality, a wholeness, that contains many roles.

The power of both the symbols and metaphors allows inner experience and change without destroying the defence systems (also see Cox and Theilgaard 1987). Thus, as we look again at the Hamlet speech quoted at the beginning of this chapter, Hamlet goes on to say:

> '.....................What would he do
> Had he the motive and cue for passion
> That I have? He would drown the stage with tears
> And cleave the general ear with horrid speech,
> Make mad the guilty and appal the free,
> Confound the ignorant, and amaze indeed
> The very faculties of eyes and ears.'
>
> *Shakespeare: Hamlet II.ii*

He is describing the chaotic and destructive outcome if the actor has indeed the real life experiences which he enacts. Hamlet is describing a loss of control of emotion that would come about if there was no distancing between the personal experience and the drama. However, towards the end of his speech, he decides on a course of action, 'the play within the play' which does create a dramatic distance, whereby it will be possible to discover the truth of his uncle's guilt. He says:

> '..........................I have heard
> That guilty creatures sitting at a play

> Have by the very cunning of the scene
> Been struck so to the soul that presently
> They have proclaimed their malefactions.
> For murder, though it hath no tongue, will speak
> With most miraculous organ. I'll have these players
> Play something like the murder of my father
> Before mine uncle. I'll observe his looks.
> I'll tent him to the quick. If 'a do blench
> I know my course.'

And then at the end of the speech he says:

> '........................The play's the thing
> Wherein I'll catch the conscience of the King.'

In dramatherapy, 'the play within the play within the play', is the point where consciences may be caught and truths revealed.

The following example illustrates how a conscious decision to work with dramatic distance brought about profound experience for the participants and the possibilities of change.

I was working with a mixed group of clients referred through an academic institution where there were problems of pressure and expectation. The students were experiencing stress from the seeming pressures being placed on them by the institution - they were nearing final exams, essays had to be in on time, folios complete, and there was a dread of their oral exam. This seemed to be a stronger theme than a fear of their written exams.

At this particular session, the group had said that it would be useful to role play the oral examination as a way of rehearsing it. As we gathered at the beginning of the group, one girl was very tearful and said that it was not only the college, she had a lot of pressure from her family. This theme focussed the group in an instant and there was a ripple round the room with an emergent theme concerning fathers and daughters. Some members said that there was a conflict about being at University because, for example, their brother had not managed to get a place; someone else said that she had traditional parents who expected her to behave as a traditional woman. The girl who was crying said that there was an additional pressure; there was expectation that if she was going to pursue an academic course then she had to do well. This was experienced as a pressure both from the father but also from the daughter herself who felt she needed to prove that she could succeed.

We could have worked psychodramatically with the individual situation of the daughter concerned, and enacted the scenes that had happened, or that needed to happen between her father and herself. She could choose a recent scene that illustrated the problem, choosing someone else from the group to play her father (and perhaps other family members); the therapist may have felt that there was early material that needed to be looked at in the girl's life and so on. It would be dealing with her life as it was happening to her, and with which other group members would identify and empathise, and through which they could perhaps play out their dramas too. This would be a perfectly valid therapeutic intervention for this situation.

I was very aware that the people in this group were facing the very real problems of their finals pressures now; my concerns were about the stirring of past history, which in its turn could trigger other material which the client, and others in the group, could find both overwhelming and also inappropriate at this particular time in their lives.

I chose to work dramatherapeutically with this group theme and decided to use dramatic material that was about father and daughter relationships, that was set in the ancient past but that would have contemporary relevance. Many themes presented themselves (Juliet and her father, from *Romeo and Juliet*; Hermia and her father from *A Midsummer Night's Dream*; Ophelia and her father from *Hamlet*). However on this occasion I chose to work with the story of Antigone and her uncle Creon:

'CREON: And are you not ashamed to act apart from them?
ANTIGONE: No; there is nothing shameful in piety to a
   brother.
CREON: Was it not a brother too that died in the opposite
   cause?
ANTIGONE: Brother by the same mother and the same sire.
CREON: Why then do you render a grace that is impious in
   his sight?
ANTIGONE: The dead man will not say that he so deems it.
CREON: Yes, if you make him but equal in honour with the
   wicked.
ANTIGONE: It was his brother, not his slave, that perished.
CREON: Wasting this land; while he fell as its champion.
ANTIGONE: Nevertheless Hades desires these rites.
CREON: But the good does not desire a like portion with the
   evil.
ANTIGONE: Who knows but this seems blameless in the
   world below?
CREON: A foe is never a friend - not even in death.
ANTIGONE: It is not my nature to join in hating, but in loving.

CREON: Pass then to the world of the dead, and if you must
needs love, love them. While I live no woman shall rule
me.'

Sophocles: Antigone

We explored the characters of Antigone, her sister Ismene, and then Antigone's
relationship with her uncle. We moved from the basic story to exploring the
characters, then the text, and improvising from the text. What evolved was an
uncle-father-daughter interaction with a chorus of uncle/fathers and a chorus of
daughters, together with an individual person as a chorus commentator (the girl who
had been crying).

This particular group were able from their own background to move readily into
the Greek play, and the understanding that resulted was more far-reaching than a
representation of their real life situations. It enabled the group to grapple with the
father-daughter and the sister relationships in a distanced scenario which made it
safe for them to explore it in depth. We agreed as a group that we were not going to
interpret the material in relation to our own families. The change in energy at the
end of this session was remarkable, and there was a general feeling in the group that
they had made decisions for themselves to come to University and that they had
always known the pressure; it was nothing new. I felt that the proximity of the
examinations had aroused feelings that had been buried for some time, and that the
women in the group felt under enormous pressure to succeed as women. It was also
useful for the men in this group to have a greater understanding of the male/female
dynamic that exists, especially around roles, relationships and expectations.

I have used the 'great themes' with all kinds of client group - one does not have
to be a graduate to experience the great truths within Shakespearian or Greek
tragedies. Further examples of this way of working will be given in the chapters on
practical application.

The above example shows how a choice of model (on this occasion, psychodrama or dramatherapy), involving greater or lesser dramatic distance, can be made
and then followed through in relation to client need.

We have seen how drama which grows from dramatic play is a part of all human
experience, whether it is the private dramas of our dreams, or the way that we
spontaneously 're-work' our experience of life. We have considered the roots of this
experience in early play development which emerges through *embodiment, projec-*
tion and *role*. We have considered the most common criticisms of drama - that it is
dangerous, that it is not real and that it can confuse people, and re-defined it within
a different reality, that of dramatic truth that is safe because of the distancing that is
established through symbol and metaphor, as well as the setting of limits and
boundaries. With this basis of the drama experience rooted in our own personal

experience and history, as well as our own culture, we are now ready to consider the basic principles which underpin dramatherapy.

The following five principles underpin our understanding of the integrated dramatherapy model:

Five basic dramatherapy principles

(i) *the paradox of the drama*: the distance that is established through the role, scene or text enables a greater depth to be explored.

(ii) *the transformative potential of the drama*: drama enables a transformation of experience and thereby enables a shift in experience of self and other.

(iii) *the symbolic nature of the drama*: whereas it is possible to work with the actual scene that happened in a person's life, dramatherapy usually works with a symbolic scene that has meaning at several levels for the person's and the group's life as a whole.

(iv) *the dramatic metaphor*: the metaphor that is embodied, projected and enacted enables profound change to take place.

(v) *the non-interpretative drama*: by consciously interpreting or offering explanations of the drama, it often blocks the continuing process of understanding which is multi-layered and multi-dimensional.

Examples of this are shown in each chapter of this book - and earlier in this chapter in the Creon/Antigone vignette.

Essentially the dramatherapy model creates a play within a play within a play - in other words, the drama within the dramatherapy group within the theatre of peoples' lives as a whole.

We only need to look at Shakespeare, for example *Hamlet* and *A Midsummer Night's Dream* to see how powerful is the play within the play. The *play within* is a point of learning, change, transformation and integration. Shakespeare's play within the play as a model for therapeutic change is the basis of my current research which I will refer to in subsequent chapters. (Its fuller exposition needs a separate publication).[6]

> 'Thus with imagined wing our swift scene flies
> In motion of no less celerity
> Than that of thought.'
>
> *Shakespeare: Henry V. III.i*

Let us voyage with an open mind and a creative imagination and remember that:

'The dramatherapy group is the empty stage which enables
these images to be represented at different levels. It symbolises
the scenario of Life itself as well as the lives of the individual
group members, and also the life of the group. Within the
context of the dramatherapy group through many forms of
dramatic expression, lives are re-created and re-presented in
symbolic form. It is the polysemic nature of dramatherapy
which enables the group's liminality to be expressed through
the multiple metaphors. Whether they are expressed
non-verbally or verbally, through role or projection, through
myth or ritual, through mask or mimesis, they are the key to our
understanding. These metaphors are the dominant symbols by
which we begin to comprehend the human condition both
specifically and generally.'

Jennings: Dramatherapy: Theory and Practice
for Teachers and Clinicians p. 14

Even as I write, I realise that this is how I see and experience it right now - soon a
new story will unfold - a new perspective - no dramatherapy treatise can be definitive
for more than a blink of a gazelle's eye.

'There are more things in heaven and earth ...
Than are dreamt of in your philosophy.'

Shakespeare: Hamlet, I.v

Chapter Two

Stages and Scripts

'A kingdom for a stage ......'

Shakespeare: Henry V. I.i

Having established in Chapter One a basic creative framework and an introduction to the dramatic reality of dramatherapy, we go on to develop a series of models for the application of dramatherapy in relation to appropriate aims and goals of the intended work. It is not sufficient for us to be convinced of the value of dramatherapeutic work and then promptly do it. It is necessary to be clear about the needs of the client, the skill that we can offer and realistic aims for the therapy itself. Furthermore, when one is working within a total service, it is important that thought is given to the relationship of the dramatherapy to the overall programme. So, for example, when I am running a dramatherapy group in an out-patients department for people with fertility problems, I need to know the medical assessment and treatment programme that people may be undergoing, the timing of any surgery, the effects of any drug treatment and the overall diagnostic and prognostic opinions. I need to have contact with the medical team, the referring consultant, and the nursing staff. I also have to be sure of a feedback structure for the fullest communication between staff members so that the client is being treated holistically and not as 'bits'. In turn, clients need to be clear about confidentiality, what is disclosed and to whom, and how decisions regarding treatment are made and sanctioned. This type of structure is not only beneficial for the patient but also supportive to the therapist so that no-one is working in isolation and without support.

Let us start by exploring the various aims of dramatherapeutic work; we shall consider them in relation to specific clients that have been referred for dramatherapy.

What can dramatherapy offer the client?

The most important irreducible fact about the drama inherent in dramatherapy is that it enables the client to get in touch with creative resources that are in themselves healing and restorative.

By freeing these resources, which are innate in everyone, it is possible to recognise and understand unhelpful past events; to identify and learn new behaviours; to re-negotiate perceptions of self and society. Furthermore, it provides pathways between our inner experience and outer reality and makes it possible to transcend ourselves and go beyond our everyday limits and boundaries.

How can this potential be translated into the realistic day-to-day work with client groups?

If we accept the basic premise of the creative dramatic resources, both in ourselves as well as for our clients, we can then look at the focus of this resource to facilitate the achievement of particular aims and goals. It is necessary for the dramatherapist to have already tapped into this resource from their own training and experience, and I will expand this in a specific chapter addressing the needs of staff (Chapter Seven). It is necessary to be aware of the person as a whole within their societal and cultural context, within which we are choosing to focus on a specific area of need. This need forms the basis of a contract between therapist and client within a therapeutic milieu. Therefore the attendance at the dramatherapy group (or individual session, see Chapter Five) becomes a creative negotiation. I emphasise the initial negotiation, because in itself it can mark a time of change, when a client may articulate their needs rather than have the therapist's objectives imposed. It is important that this is seen as a negotiation, because realistic expectations may then be acknowledged rather than therapist or client having unrealistic aims of each other. I shall develop the framework for referral and diagnostic procedures towards the end of this chapter. Let us now look at the various models within which we may apply dramatherapy methods.

How is a model of practice identified?

A model of practice needs to state the prime focus of the therapy and the structure which enables it to take place. Such a structure is governed by time, space and duration and is underpinned by appropriate methodology. For example, a group which is focussed on acquiring communication skills would not use methods to explore the person's inner life. A model of practice in dramatherapy enables us to be clear about a working structure of dramatherapy application. Dramatherapy itself is a diverse and complex discipline with a plethora of methods and range of stimuli. Without a model we are in danger of running an activities session of drama that is unfocussed and unconnected. By unfocussed I mean that it has not been thought through in terms of having relevance to the particular needs of an individual and group at a particular time. By unconnected I mean that it is not 'in context' of the client's life as a whole. Therefore a magic box of techniques that we might or might not apply is inappropriate to practice. The need for a clear model is perhaps even more essential to dramatherapy because of its very diversity. As we saw in Chapter One, a simple definition is almost impossible for a potentially ungraspable medium. In many psychotherapies, the psychotherapy itself is defined by the model. For example, analytic group psychotherapy[1] will of itself define the theoretical model of the group which may be applied to a specific population. This model gives guidelines for the time and duration of the group, numbers of group members, the emergence and understanding of certain phenomena and the procedures for dealing with them. Physical space and human bodies are held constant in a circular shape for the unfolding of the group's process and individuals' life stories.

However, since dramatherapy involves various methods which physically, emotionally, mentally and spiritually mobilise the client, care has to be taken that the method itself does not become the model. The methods used are appropriate to a model.

Since drama is intrinsic to the human experience and is part of our essential development and evolution as people, drama itself is the means whereby inner change and therefore outer change can be brought about. How this is achieved will depend on the model of practice of dramatherapy that is adopted.

The following models of dramatherapy practice are guides and should not be treated as rigid formulae.

1. Creative expressive

The focus is on the undeveloped healthy aspects of people and this model encourages them to discover their own creative energy. Creative drama structures are used to expand people's awareness and stimulate their imagination. The model is intended to increase confidence and encourage people to be articulate. Co-operation and negotiation skills are inherent in this type of group because for it to be successful, people need to work together in order to create a piece of drama. Therefore many social skills may be learned through a creative group even though it is not the prime focus of the model. It is appropriate to use the whole range of dramatic and theatre methods (some of which are described in Chapter Three) and it is important to start *within* the skills and experience of the group members. It is usual to commence with movement and sound, building up the more flexible use of the body and voice. The capacity to risk-take will gradually emerge when participants realise that they are not being made to look foolish. This model of group does not focus on particular life problems or aim to work with specific pathology. It is important for it to be non-interpretive and to allow the creative process itself to generate energy.

It is often necessary to make participants familiar with basic drama (therapy) methods in body and voice - there may therefore be a didactic phase at the beginning of the group.

I will discuss starting points together with methodology in greater detail in Chapter Three. However it is a good guideline, if in doubt, to work with the developmental paradigm - embodiment, projection, role - described in Chapter One. Work on primary sensation through the human body and simple movement is crucial before any role work is undertaken. The creative-expressive model can be compared with the multi-media play stage of the child, where a person explores the potential of their body and voice in order to facilitate the imagination. It is helpful to remember that the training of the actor starts with the body and most theatre directors emphasise the importance of the discipline achieved through a movement programme.[2]

Scenario: a community based group for former psychiatric patients

I have been asked to work in a club for people who have been in a psychiatric hospital for varying lengths of time and who are now living in the community: some working, others managing to live independently in the community. It is not a treatment setting; rather it is run as a therapeutic community which meets once a week and has a structure based on a large community group, together with small art, music and drama therapy groups and a large movement group. Each of the arts therapies has its regular population and everyone attends the community meeting which starts off the evening. A large number stay on for the movement group. Although each of the arts therapies has a stable population, each group has a few people who move between all three and others are encouraged to move when it is felt they are ready for new experiences. There is a good communication between all the staff who are committed long-term and therefore able to provide a stable framework for the work. All the staff attend the community meeting and many join in the movement group. The staff consists of psychiatric and social work staff and a team of arts therapists in music, drama and art, and instructors in movement and dance. There is a support system for individual patients as well as for the large group.

When I first started work there, the drama group had been run very much as an evening class in drama with structured voice and drama exercises and reading of plays. This provided a secure framework and gave the group a focussed way of working. There had been no attempt at improvisation or the development of thematic work.

Thinking through

Since there was already an established 'culture' to this group I want to build on what they already have; my considerations are that the group seems oversafe and tends to be repetitive in how the members use the drama work. I am conscious that there will be thoughts and feelings about me coming as the new person, especially since I am considerably younger than the last encumbant. I therefore decide to free-wheel for a few weeks and see where the group is prepared to go.

Possible plan: I would ask the group to describe the work they have already done in the sessions and encourage them to *show it actively*. I must allow time for them to explore what I have on offer and the limits of my skills and experience .... scripts to improvise perhaps?

I discuss with them my aims of developing the work they have already done and using improvisation as well as scripted work. (I have a covert aim which I do not share until later which is to encourage them as a group to go to the theatre and be able to discourse about what they see *and to be critical*.)

This group can be described as a slow open group with a hard core of regular members which from time to time integrates new people that come into the centre as well as those who had decided to attend from other groups.

After these initial 'casing' weeks, I begin to develop a framework of body and voice work which starts with developing: spatial awareness, private and public space, relaxation, testing of spatial proximity, breathing, voice production, articulation. It is important to allow time for comment and feedback on the experiences. The group is composed of a variety of personalities:

    (i) the hard traditional core that has been with the group for a long time and whose members often dominate the conversations;

    (ii) several silent withdrawn people who rarely speak;

    (iii) some who are still on maintenance medication;

    (iv) those who attend outpatient psychotherapy groups;

    (v) a few who attended all the day centres and social clubs available.

I was clear that my brief should be to work with the creative process of the drama.

From my notebook

There are many issues in the group about trust and dependency and whether the members can trust the other people or myself; there is a tendency for the group to feel at times like a club with long attendance as a sign of hierarchy, and I feel that one of my aims should be to encourage more autonomy. The voice production sessions are also helped by the music therapist who works musically with the group on their breathing and vocal power.

As the group become used to working with me, and we have done some preparatory physical and vocal work, I introduce some drama games to focus on group dynamics and give more confidence for them to function as a group. It is important not to let it become a *chat group* which is the tendency for those people who want an up-date on the news and gossip. (Me still nervous at wanting to change things!)

After the games some simple improvisation starters - e.g. 'You are waiting at the bus queue when ...'

Situations within the everyday life that can be tackled by three people and worked into a scene - try to establish pair-work in the voice and movement and then progress to relationships through which people work together in threes and deal with the dynamics of the three instead of the pair. (Often the first struggle that a couple have when a new baby arrives.) There are many issues around families and feelings of being ostracised with families being blamed for their difficulties. Yet it is not appropriate to engage in exploration of this material in a direct way - scripts?

I will describe more of this group later in the chapter after discussing other models of practice.

Brief resumé of the creative expressive model

Aim:	to develop latent resources of the client through creative drama.
Methods:	all drama and theatre approaches within the capacity of the client, taking contra-indications into account.
Time:	one to two hours per week depending on the concentration span of the group; (for example, with people who are severely learning disabled, forty minutes may be more appropriate).
Numbers:	varying depending on client disability; necessity for a regular core into which new members may be integrated.
Structure:	either 'closed' group or 'slow open' group.
Setting:	psychiatric or rehabilitative day centre; probation and after-care programme; community home or hostel.
Client group:	a broad range can benefit from this type of group including those with learning disabilities; social and behavioural problems; self-help groups.

2. Tasks and skills

Drama is an important way of rehearsing and practising the skills we need in everyday life. It is a way of 'trying something on for size' and we can observe role-testing behaviour in everyday life, for example in the play of young children and in adolescent changes in self-presentation. In societies where there is a clear expectation of adult behaviour and families too, the everyday norms are learnt through the modelling of adult roles and through initiation ceremonies. Children grow up with a clear prescription of how they are expected to behave. In societies where there is a looser social fabric and ideas of choice, then greater experimentation takes place. In all situations, the adult role-models and society's expectations are lasting factors in how the emergent adult will behave.

Part of this development is concerned with social convention and etiquette such as appropriate forms of greeting, dress and social discourse. It becomes more elaborated when people become aware of the implications of their behaviour, their capacity to change the outcome of situations through careful negotiation and sensitive communication skills. We can observe in the media the emphasis placed on public image and self-presentation and how well-known personalities change their voices, gestures and dress.

Many good social skills programmes are run by occupational therapists and social psychologists which aim to improve communication. The dramatherapist has particular skills to contribute in this area because of the repertoire of dramatic methods that can be utilised. For example, social skills can be improved by dramatising a scene to anticipate situations that people will encounter in everyday life (Jennings 1988). Generally speaking, task orientated dramatherapy works with situations that are unfamiliar; (perhaps a person has been hospitalised for a long period of time), or with situations that have to be re-learned because the initial learning is inappropriate. The emphasis is not on the underlying effect but on the behaviours themselves.

Scenario: a group of women who are attending a support group before having major surgery

There is anxiety and tension and a feeling of not knowing what to expect; will they be the same afterwards, will it hurt, will their partners still find them attractive? There is an emergent theme of 'I didn't like to bother the doctor; I didn't want to waste his time; he is so busy'. The group say there is much information that they would have liked to have had from their doctor only they did not like to ask, and also that much of what the doctor said they did not understand and that they did not like to admit it. We decide on two courses of action. One is to ask the clinic nurse to come and give a talk and then answer any questions that are bothering the women; the second is to explore communication skills with doctors so that in the future they may feel more confident in asking what they need to know. The conversation veers off in many directions as people get pent up feelings off their chest, 'You never see the same person twice, they don't treat you like a person, all this waiting ....' I bring the group back to its focus, which is very specific. How can we communicate with the doctor when:

1. we have not understood what he or she has said and
2. we need more information?

I take an example from one of the group member's recent experiences; she had a vaginal examination and the doctor had told her she would need a D and C; she had heard this as a di-ency. She hadn't liked to ask further and her neighbour, when she got home, thought the doctor might mean a scrape. She was equally worried by each; the first because she did not know what it was, and she thought it might mean cancer; the second, because it sounded painful and they might scrape her womb away. The group want to pitch in with all their ideas about what it was and again I have to keep it in focus. It is important to role-model the finding out of information whether I already know it or not, so we look up the meaning of D and C, 'dilatation and curettage' and a description of what it is. (A brief list of useful information books is essential; it may be that in your group it is not just book information that is needed, but *where* to find out certain information - e.g. Citizens Advice Bureau, Birth Registry, etc.)

This may sound a simple piece of intervention but several things are taking place:

1. I must not collude with the image of being all knowing;
2. there are ways and means of finding things out;
3. there are certain issues about which we should have facts rather than speculation;
4. there is no loss of face at not knowing something.

Having ascertained these facts, we are now able to set up the context of the doctor/patient interview. I ask the same group member to help set up the scene as it actually happened, and we create an acting area in the middle of the group. There is a desk where the doctor sits, and lots of papers, a telephone on the desk, the nurse is busy at the trolley. Slowly the scenario takes shape and she chooses people to play the doctor and the nurse. I ask her where the door leads to and she says into the corridor outside where there is a whole line of people waiting, so she feels even more guilty about taking up too much time. The rest of the group sit in a line on chairs as the waiting patients and I ask her to take it from the point after the examination when she has re-dressed. I ask her to sit in the doctor's chair and say what he said. I ask her to enact it as it had happened. She sits down, looks at the papers and says, as the doctor:

Doctor: Mrs Smith, I've examined you down below and you need
               a di-ency.

(I check with her and ask whether the doctor said 'down below' and she thinks for a moment and says, 'Well maybe it was "inside"; he'd taken a look inside. Does it matter?' I suggest that we try to create the scene as accurately as possible and then see if it is possible to change it. Mrs Smith goes back to her role as patient and the scene re-runs.)

Doctor:	Mrs Smith, I have examined you inside and you need a D and C.
Mrs Smith:	When will that be doctor?
Doctor:	We'll send you an appointment, probably in a few months' time.

(Mrs Smith gets up and leaves the room.)

I suggest to Mrs Smith that she plays the role of herself and I ask another group member to volunteer to play the doctor and change anything she wants to.

Doctor:	Mrs Smith I have examined your insides and you need a D and C.
Mrs Smith:	A what?
Doctor:	A D and C; dilatation and curettage. We take out some of your womb.

I stop the role-play as several group members shake their heads and one of them says 'You make it sound like a hysterectomy'. We continued to explore these few lines of dialogue so that the patient feels comfortable asking for an explanation. Mrs Smith then takes on the patient role again and is able to ask the doctor for an explanation and then some follow-up questions.

We then looked at language and wrote up all the different terms, both medical and popular that were in common usage. This gave the group some confidence in being able to understand what the doctor said. Most importantly this session built up the confidence to be able to ask when they did *not* understand something.

(A spin off from this group was that everyone knew more about their anatomy, myself included!)

Brief resumé of the task centred model

Aim:	to achieve skills in communication, confidence and social interaction, self-presentation.
Methods:	voice and movement, role-play and simulation.
Time:	One and a half hours per week for fixed period of time, eg six weeks or 12 weeks.
Numbers:	eight to twelve
Structure:	closed group - fixed population.

Setting: all settings - institution, community, rehabilitation, after-care.

Client group: most, but consideration to be given to social skill needs of
                  particular populations.

3. Psychotherapeutic model

Dramatherapy provides the methodology through which a psychotherapeutically
orientated group is conducted. The therapist is trained both in psychotherapy and
drama(therapy) and makes use of the drama to highlight psychotherapeutic phenomena and process when appropriate.

   Dramatherapy is not necessarily a psychotherapy in the narrow definition of the
term, unless one takes a broad view that all therapies that work towards personal
change are psychotherapies. This, I maintain, renders the term so broad that it
becomes meaningless. Most therapeutic intervention has psychotherapeutic elements - acknowledged or otherwise - but that does not make it psychotherapy.

   The focus is on insight and change within the psychotherapeutic milieu, working
with transferences, introjection and projection. Individual and group processes (see
also Chapter Five, dramatherapy with individuals) are the vehicle through which
intra-psychic change can happen and thereby external behaviours modified. The
drama psychotherapist may interpret symbols and behaviour where relevant and
makes direct use of the transference relationship to explore past situations.

*Scenario: A group of men and women attending a therapeutic community where the
week is structured into different sorts of groups*

All members of the group are part of the larger community (non-residential) and the
week is structured into large community group, small groups which meet twice
weekly, activity groups, option therapy groups (music, art therapy etc.), meetings
and workshops. The focus of therapeutic change is the small group. There is a
multi-professional staff team including psychotherapists, arts therapists, group
leaders with particular skills, and instructors.

   This group has been meeting for six weeks in a twice weekly group, for one and
a half hours at 11 am each Tuesday and Thursday. There has been a lot of 'shaking
down', testing of group boundaries, challenging of leadership.

Tuesday session in the seventh week:

Group member   i.   This is just a waste of time

                 ii. We're not doing anything.

Therapist		What does the group want to do?
	i.	*(Mimicking)* What does the group want? You make me sick.
	iii.	Who's a good actor then?
	ii.	He's not acting - he means it.
	i.	'Course I bloody mean it.
	iii.	What do you mean?
	i.	I mean...I'm fed up with sitting around... therapy is just middle class.
	vi.	Speak for yourself - you with the O levels.
	vii.	I've got O levels too, do you mind? and A levels...
	v.	Bully for you, *(rounding on therapist)* I suppose you've got degrees as well...

(*Teaching point*: the group is highly articulate and volatile; the challenges and anger are quite apparent; there is no need at this point for dramatherapeutic intervention).

	i.	What do you know about people like us?
	vii.	She's a person too.
	i.	You could have fooled me - just sitting there the ice-maiden.
Group members	i. ii. & v.	*all smirk.*
	iii. iv. & vii.	*look uncomfortable.*
	vi. & viii.	*look helpless.*
Therapist		Some people look helpless and some triumphant - shall we go on playing winners and losers?
	iv.	*(with relief)* How do you play?
Therapist		Well, we seem to be playing it already, but the winners are only winning and the losers losing - perhaps people could share both sides of themselves.
	v.	I've never won anything.
	vi.	*(after a silence)* I only wanted to win approval.
	iv.	You've got to win - my dad said - when I was at school.

The hot theme which emerges from this group is 'approval' and everyone has childhood and adolescent experiences of expectations that they felt they could not live up to - joining a gang to get peer approval - no win - can't win - give up; transferentially I am the parent who has expectations of them in the group and it is necessary for them to be able to articulate this towards me, and equally necessary for me to hold on.

(*Teaching point*: the dramatic possibilities for this scene are many - we could psychodramatise actual incidents from peoples' lives; re-enact scenes between parents and children. We could stay with the process in the containment of the circle and the words, or we could dramatise a group theme - (one of the Nordic or Russian stories comes to mind when princes or children have to prove themselves to get approval) - this is the scanning by the *internal supervisor* (elaborated in Chapter Three) that monitors the therapist's intervention. My scanning re-inforces my intuition to stay with the present and not to intervene to change mode, at least for the present.)

i.	I was just never good enough - as anybody. *(he looks as if he could cry).*
Therapist:	So who was the ice-maiden?
i.	*(Starts to cry)*, Mum of course, cold and distant.
iii.	*(Puts a hand on i's shoulder and he flinches)*
i.	Sorry - thought you were going to hit me - big boys mustn't cry.
iii.	*(Goes to withdraw hand)*
i.	No - leave it there - but don't let it get heavy - no more pressure.

(*Teaching point*: the drama is there in the group's movement, body and role - there is no need to impose additional technique. My internal artist already sees the dramatic scenario unfolding - limits of time and space are well grounded - i.e. the same room, same time, one and a half hours, sitting in the circle. The internal therapist holds on to the transferential image of parent with unyielding expectations - many of them unrealistic - and resists the counter-transference to respond as if they are children. On some occasions it could be useful to share this with a group if they are stuck - 'I wonder why I feel like a frustrated parent right now?')

Brief resumé of the psychotherapeutic model

Aim:	to bring about intra-psychic change and more healthy functioning in relationships.

Methods:	specific techniques when appropriate to material being presented - usually triggered transferentially.
Time:	one per week (on average).
Numbers:	usually eight or ten people.
Structure:	closed, with agreed time for opening to integrate new people.
Setting:	day-centre, hospital, therapeutic community, private practice.
Client group:	those who would normally be referred for group psychotherapy including those with a range of neuroses, obsessive behaviour, dependence, addictions.

4. The integrated model

This model of practice could be said to integrate the previous three. It is the purest model of dramatherapy where the focus is on the healing properties of the drama itself within the therapy. It is the most recent model of practice to emerge within the vast range of methods and structures, and is the least written about. The historical reason for this is given in the Introduction and Chapter One.

Although one may choose to grasp this model through psychotherapeutic analysis, it is only one way of viewing this multi-dimensional, multi-metaphoric phenomenon. It can equally be assessed through a theatre (eg Stanislavski/Brecht) analysis. The danger of any single interpretation is that it becomes, in itself, self-limiting and robs the medium of its wholeness by concentrating on its parts. Dramatic healing dramas and rituals existed in 'spaces set apart' since time archaic, speaking to the integrated person and society through symbols and actions, through all the arts and representations. Drama, like the unconscious, is timeless and is as relevant to the human condition now as it was thousands of years ago. It responds to the fundamental needs in people to act, to enact, to re-enact, to re-work, as well as to discover, to risk, to voyage. Even though we may be 'tempest tossed' we may also be aware of the 'fall of the sparrow'.

The integrated model may be appropriate within the widest variety of settings. It puts the greatest demands both on client and therapist alike, and care must be taken in selection and assessment of people. The dramatherapist needs to be thoroughly trained in all forms of theatre, to have a well developed creative imagination, to have opportunities to practice his or her art form, as well as having experienced their own personal psychotherapy and training, and have appropriate supervision with an imaginative supervisor.

Although of wide application, there may be limitations in the setting that make other models of dramatherapy more appropriate. It is a creative organisation that can allow the true healing power of the arts to flourish in therapy, that can allow growth of a medium as society itself changes, that can acknowledge something in the now for its truth and beauty but realise that next week, next month or next year, it may have changed, moved on, or appear transformed.

The key concept in understanding the integrated, 'pure' dramatherapy is its transformative power, and the transformations are limitless. We may come to a pause, a rest on the journey, but the continuing path is there whether it is visible or not. The path is a humbling one, because although the dramatherapist may facilitate, structure, push, or hold back, essentially she or he is a channel through which creative energy may be linked. The creative dramatic process is a mysterious one, it is elusive, and time out to reflect is essential for it to stay in touch. The guru does not have a place here since there must be movement through the shadows as the great story unfolds. If we as dramatherapists can contribute the smallest part to the unfolding of the stories then the journey is worth while.

The group described in Chapter Four is a clear example of the integrated model. The following scenario also serves.

Scenario: A training group meeting to work with their own material within the dramatherapeutic mode.

The group have been together for over two years, and this group is the core of their training experience which also includes lectures, seminars, workshops and practice.

There are 12 trainees in the group, eight women and four men. They come from a variety of backgrounds, including theatre, psychology, nursing, occupational therapy, social work, teaching, and community arts.

The group starts in its established way of feed-back from the last time they met, checking out material that was stimulated by the session (which worked on a Bushman myth about the lady from the stars, re-told by Laurens van der Post in *The Heart of the Hunter*).[3] Two members of the group wish to share dreams they have had on themes from the myth, another member has suffered a bereavement within the close family. There are many images concerning death and endings, and I suggest it cannot be co-incidental that this group is meeting the week before Easter. One group member, who has been silent up until now, suddenly says, 'but Easter is also about new beginnings'. The group goes silent, and she says 'I've got a story to tell, if I may'.

The summary of her story (preserving total anonymity), is that since the group last met, she had received information about her real mother. She had been adopted as a baby, told of her adoption as a child, felt she had adjusted to it very well and had never made a secret of it to her friends. She says that in her teens she had fantasies concerning her 'real' parents, sometimes her father and at other times her mother.

Although very happy with her adoptive parents, she felt very wistful when wondering about her own parents, and decided to trace them if possible. The social worker had told her that there had been no contact with her natural parents since the adoption, and her original birth certificate gave her mother's name and her occupation as none; it said 'father unknown'. However, there was now more recent information and her mother had been traced to a village in the north; she had married and had a teen-age family. The woman now felt in a dilemma about whether to pursue it any further, she was concerned about all the issues involved in raking up the past, how her mother would feel, and so on, but at the same time having a real desire to know about her father.

When she had summarised the story, a member of the group asked her what she wanted to do - did she want to explore some issues in the group? She said she did, but did not know what. Someone said that perhaps she wanted to see what she might say to her mother, another said that perhaps she needed to explore the decision itself. She looked at me, quite helpless, and said 'what do you think?'

(*Teaching point*: How does one respond to a direct question? Usually answering it directly brings an interaction to a close, not to answer at all is artificial. How then can one answer in a way that is facilitating to the process? My feeling on this occasion was that she was asking for help to clarify some of her confused feelings and conflicts before she could even make a decision, or several decisions.)

Therapist: Everything sounds very confused to me at the moment and maybe the group feels confused too.

What do you mean, confused - we just want to help - she needs some help - surely we can do something - it's an unfinished story - and who knows who her dad might be - maybe a gypsy.

Therapist: Exactly - we are already inventing her story for her, and lost parents become romantic for us all!

Group member i. That's how I felt as a teenager, but I am also very angry - at being given away. I know I have lovely parents and I'm loved and looked after - but I was given away - why?

Therapist: Do you have any factual information?

i. Well my mother was very young, seventeen. She is now a teacher, so maybe she was still at school - maybe parental pressure ...

(*Teaching point*: my intuition tell me that she is experiencing the same dilemma concerning whether to find her mother, as her mother did over her adoption).

> iii.   At least you were allowed to be born - I had an
>   abortion in my teens, and I still feel guilty.

The group are very subdued and look around as if expecting further painful revelations; they are rewarded.

> iv.   So I was adopted as well - and I don't want to know
>   who my parents are - I hate them anyway - and my
>   adopted parents - I've left them all and am going it alone.

(*Teaching point*: There comes a moment in a group's life, what I call a *groundswell*, when it feels as if there is a common core of why a group has come together - previously undisclosed and sometimes forgotten, common experiences. For example, in one group I worked with, six out of the eight members had been sent to boarding school while the parents went abroad; in another group, over half the group had close relatives that had died violently. Dramatherapeutically, these major themes can be worked with, in the group as a whole, often drawing on epic and mythic structures; my own imagination is bringing to mind Moses in the bulrushes, the judgement of Solomon, the *Mahabharata*. I choose to take a pulse of where the group is with their imagination).

Therapist: What do you feel these stories are about?

                        Choices - decisions - being abandoned - guilt - feeling
                        helpless - uncertainty - anger - punishment - forgiveness -
                        feeling torn - wanting a baby - wanting to be a baby -
                        wanting to be a parent - fear - loss -

Therapist: Several of these words and phrases could be grouped
                        together - I'm going to suggest that in three spaces of the
                        room we place a phrase - being abandoned, decisions,
                        forgiveness. Will people please go the space where they
                        identify with a phrase right now.

Some people walk immediately to a space; others stop and pause; others walk to a space and then go to another. I suggest they try each place and then decide. One or two people say that they already know - the others move around, pause for a moment and then choose; we end up with the following grouping:

Being abandoned:	one man and three women.
Decisions:	two men and two women.
Forgiveness:	three women and one man.
Therapist:	Each group take a large piece of paper and brain-storm all the associations you have with your phrase.

(*Teaching point*: large pieces of paper that several people can work on is essential - like the sheets of a flip chart - together with a variety of crayons and felt pens).

The small groups work with a lot of energy, talking, writing and drawing symbols.

Therapist:	Will you now, as a group, see what story, play or myth you associate with what you have written?

There is some discussion and debate as several ideas are tossed around and thoughts risked.

(*Teaching point*: it is important that people can risk ideas without fear of ridicule and also that they can be generous enough to let go of an idea and not to insist that it be pursued.)

My own undisclosed Biblical thoughts have some synchronicity with the group. The stories they choose are:

Being abandoned:	*Moses in the Bullrushes*.
Decisions:	*The Judgement of Solomon*.
Forgiveness:	Hermia and Egeus from *A Midsummer Night's Dream*.

(*Teaching point*: the therapist needs to exercise caution concerning the point of entry in a story or myth; the above scenarios could yield lengthy dramatisation that may not necessarily be helpful. My intuition suggests that the crux of the stories is the time before these stories happened. It is a useful structure to say to oneself 'is this material Act Two or Three? What is Act One about, or the prologue, or the programme notes?')

Therapist:	These three stories tell the story of the resolution of the conflict. Let's start some time before. How do these tales begin? You can place it in whatever historical time you like.

The groups start discussing, turn to me for historical accuracy and I suggest that they work with what they can remember. There is a high degree of involvement and not much 'talking about' but preliminary role work.

Therapist: You have 15 minutes to work at a scene that culminates
                              in these stories.

The groups continue to work at experimentation in role - they are used to working from the where, when, who, what and why. What results is the following. They make use of props and large pieces of cloth from the wardrobe. All three groups are set in the past.

The 'decision' group choose to go first: two couples.
The scene is the relationship between a pregnant woman and her husband and a barren woman and her husband. The two women used to be friends; now pregnant, the first woman is full of joy and expectation and her friend is envious; she follows her around getting more and more bitter; she talks to her husband about feeling unfulfilled and starts to blame him for the fact that they have no child.

   In Scene Two, the barren woman plans to steal the baby and insist that it was always hers. She comes in the middle of the night and steals it from the house and sits on the step singing to it. Then there is a knock on the door - (the scene moved several group members to tears).

The 'being abandoned' group present Moses' mother.
They ask the remainder of the group to represent the chorus of midwives who chant below their breaths - 'and kill the boys, and kill the boys'; the chorus of huntsmen who shout - 'and kill what we find, and kill what we find' - and then a chorus of mothers who say - 'sail away, sail away to the promised land'.

   Moses' mother is pregnant and overhears with her friends the edict that the midwives must kill all boys at birth - chorus - she steals away and gives birth in the forest; she hides her child and returns to look after it; she hears the huntsmen in the distance - chorus - and realises she must get the child away to safety; she and her sister create a cradle and place the child in the water; the mothers in the village echo her blessing on the child.

The third group present the conflict between Egeus and Hermia.
When her father insists she marries Demetrius or be banished, she runs away with Lysander to the forest where they encounter other-world-creatures. They both get lost but find each other and marry before returning home to ask forgiveness from Egeus.

The group, both as audience and participants, were very moved by the stories and we structured a feed-back in role -

— *as Egeus:* I only thought I was doing what was right and proper - I wanted to protect my daughter.

— *as Moses' mother:* I had to give him away - to save him.

— *as the barren woman:* I am consumed with jealousy - it devours me and I cannot think of anything else.

— *as Moses:* I have to trust her.

Therapist: Choose any of the characters from the scenes and
                             describe your journey in the first person; put as
                             much description in as you can; end the story with a
                             statement about what you have learnt on the way.

The group had 15 minutes to write their stories and then shared within the group the last few lines about what they had learnt.

The group's absorption and mood can be summed up by the statement from the girl who had had the abortion;

'As the barren woman, I have learned that I must forgive myself before I can forgive anyone else.'

We can see that all these three stories have overlapping themes that include loss, fear, conflict, judgements - all the phrases that the group had originally suggested.

The woman who had told her story said 'it's given me a lot to think about - at least my decision won't be an angry one'. She had played Moses' mother but had written her story as Moses the baby - ending with 'I have to trust her'.

Brief resumé of integrated model

Aims: to stimulate latent creativity, metaphoric processes and
                   mimesis; healing at a deeper level.

Methods: the fullest range of drama/theatre/literary/mythic structures.

Time: Two hours regular meeting - days/week-ends intermittently.

Numbers: eight to fifteen; occasionally larger groups.

Structure: depends on group membership - weekly/monthly.

Setting: most where there is supportive ethos.

Client group: people reasonably habituated to dramatherapy and principles;
                  sometimes can be used as a progression from other models;
                  trainees; actors.

In this chapter I have illustrated several models of dramatherapy practice - they are
not exhaustive and new ways of working are constantly developing. Some practitioners use a systemic approach, for example, others base their work within a
particular theoretical framework, such as that of Jung.

These models of practice are not rigid or exclusive. They have a particular focus
that may be right for a group at a particular time. The focus nevertheless needs
structuring in time, space, duration and intent, but the focus can shift when appropriate.

The dramatherapist is a frontiersperson waiting at the threshold of intervention
and containing and holding what needs to be expressed.

Chapter Three

Mainsprings and Methods

The lunatic, the lover, the poet
Are of imagination all compact.
One sees more devils than vast hell can hold.
That is the madman. The lover, all as frantic,
Sees Helen's beauty in a brow of Egypt.
The poet's eye, in a fine frenzy rolling,
Doth glance from heaven to earth, from earth to heaven.
And as imagination bodies forth
The forms of things unknown, the poet's pen
Turns them to shapes, and gives to airy nothing
A local habitation and a name.

Shakespeare: A Midsummer Night's Dream, V.i

I describe the dramatherapist as a channel; it is a two way channel, shaped like a spiral through which creative experiences move through unconscious and conscious processes at the service of the client and group. It brings to mind the image of the sufi, circling on an axis, with one arm raise to the heavens and one to the earth; or the Temiar belief that healing forces come through one's spirit guide in dreams, and are translated by the shaman into practice at healing seances through ritual, music, dance and drama. Dramatherapists draw on personal life experiences that have been assimilated through training and practice and continue to develop from their own creativity, practice and supervisory guide. I shall discuss more fully the role of the dramatherapist in Chapter Seven, and here focus on the dramatherapeutic presence. We saw in the last chapter how we can understand dramatherapy through several models, but how does this work *in situ*?

First of all we need to be aware of the internal states of the dramatherapist that need to be kept in balance, and constantly nurtured and stimulated. They have different and complementary functions and all are necessary. Some are present in other forms of therapy but the dramatherapist *per se* needs to develop and be aware of them all.

The internal patient

The internal patient brings together those aspects of ourselves that have made similar journeys to those of our clients and patients. We too have suffered pain and loss, conflict and blocks, made destructive decisions, caused hurt, destroyed instead of creating, been lost - not only in the past but as part of our evolution as a *human* being. Our own personal therapy, which may well take several forms, has helped us to understand ourselves better, but we do not come to a full stop. As Peter Hall said recently in a television interview of Peter Brook,

> 'It is one of his unique qualities that he can make mistakes -
> can get it wrong.'

We live in a society where the emphasis is always on getting it right - prescriptive living is an over-arching ethos that permeates schools, work settings and domestic life. Experimenting and risk-taking are not encouraged (we only have to look at the new curriculum for schools to see how it lacks adventure), therefore for the most part we keep within a narrow range of experience and live up to expectations of others. We forget that this is precisely what our patients are struggling with and through therapy we hope to assist them to find equilibrium. It is our own *internal patient* that has some insight but continues to be human, that *connects* with the client. We may not be conscious of the connection at the time, or we may get an 'ouch, I've been there too' feeling. The danger is that the connection can turn into identification and *get in the way* of working on the client's behalf. It is my inner core of suffering that connects with the client's suffering that will help me keep my humanity in the therapeutic endeavour. It is not enough in itself, to function adequately as a dramatherapist.

The internal therapist

The internal therapist brings the whole range of therapeutic knowledge and under-standing to bear on the situation. It presents choices of possible ways of working, it scans a range of intervention and weighs up an appropriate intervention. It checks out the responses of the internal patient. The internal therapist is not just a logical, left-hemisphere entity, it too has a balance of intuition and imagination together with hard core knowledge and experience. It reminds the dramatherapist of transference phenomena about which the internal patient might be distressed - it helps the internal patient both to understand any distress and to use it usefully at a personal and professional level.

The internal therapist takes executive action on behalf of the individual or group, for example by insistence on certain limits and boundaries, by making decisions concerning referral and appropriateness of group membership.

The dramatherapist has internalised, through training and further education, a wide range of theories, from educational, clinical and social and anthropological stances, and is more sympathetic to some than others. Nevertheless, this broad spectrum must be at a state of readiness, to inform the practitioner (see Chapter Seven on professional identity), and clarify appropriate decisions concerning intervention. Just as the internal patient needs continued sustenance, the internal therapist needs continued development through courses, workshops, reading, and through taking on new challenges in relation to practice.

The internal supervisor

The internal supervisor grows and matures with practice. It is facilitated by the supervision we have had in training and as practitioners. It is not, as many become trapped by, the internal judge and critic. These internalised states, when unhelpful, belong to the internal patient. The internal supervisor is able to stand a little apart and look in. Across the river bank[1] seems to me the right metaphoric distance; on the river bank the supervisor is able to see the water and the shore, the depths and the shallows, the swift current and the calm pools, and very importantly, is able to throw a life-line when one is in difficulty. The internal supervisor monitors the therapeutic process *in situ*, and stabilises the relationship between the internal therapist and patient (rather in the same way as the external supervisor has a monitoring and stabilising role between ourselves and our patients).

It is useful, as our internal supervisor develops, to use as role models other helpful and informed people, whose style, opinions and practice we respect. This slowly synthesises with our experience of supervising others, our own individual and unique style, into a potent and helpful dimension of our work. In time, the internal supervisor works smoothly alongside our other internalised states, but is also in readiness to be called up for emergencies, to review, or when we feel more stuck than our clients.

The internal creative artist

The internal artist has always been a part of us even though it may have been neglected, undernourished or ignored. It is an essential part of the dramatherapist and is not just that part of us which is creative, but that part that has developed our art form extensively and *continues to do so*. The dramatherapist before or during training needs to have been actor, director and playwright - and preferably choreographer and scenic designer as well. It is the art form of the drama that forms the bedrock of our dramatherapy work, and it is not enough to have read about it and done a few workshops. It is essential that the dramatherapist has taken part in drama and theatre training through voice, movement, improvisation and performance, and has, as well, directed others. Otherwise we are never able to use our drama therapeutically in the fullest sense - we may be well practised in techniques of games and role play, have a hundred warm-up ideas to draw upon, but the dramatherapist is not merely a technician. The dramatherapist is a practising artist at all levels, and draws upon personal artistic experience and aesthetics in practice. The internal artist informs all the other internal states - patient, therapist and supervisor as well as existing in its own right. It is often the creative impulse that enables the supervisor to help the drama to move on, it assists the therapist in dramatic content and structure; it can connect with the internal patients, especially in despair and find creative ways through the morass.

Nevertheless, the internal artist is also a creature of many moods - and may spark with a whirlwind of ideas or be sunk in the gloom of the pit. The artist needs the other internalised states in order to be of the greatest help to the patient, but the greatest strength is usually the impetus to break through repetitive cycles. It is the action when we shake the kaleidoscope and all patterns fall again in new groupings and shapes.

It is also the resource for much of our creative dramatic methodology and thematic material. I have written earlier (Jennings 1986) on the difference it made in my practice to read *Henry VI*, and play the role of Queen Margaret - having ordered the death of Rutland, I dip a napkin in his blood and fling it in the face of his father York while I taunt him. I am the person whom York calls 'she-wolf of France'.

The effect on me continued long after the playing of the part; it enabled me to be in touch with my most base, murderous and destructive self, to believe in the part as I was ordering the slaughter of the child and having my hands wet with its blood; this did far more for my self-awareness, humility and growth, than many years of psycho-analysis.

In Chapter Seven, I will draw more on these resources for the dramatherapist, illustrating the dangers of only stimulating our creativity for our work, and not letting it also exist for ourselves.

With our four internal states prepared, let us journey further and look at some essentials for dramatherapy practice.

A referral system

The temptation, especially for the new practitioner, is to work with all comers; glad of referral and affirmation from colleagues, we accept all those who are sent our way. This is less the case than 20 years ago when dramatherapy was a marginal activity in hospitals and schools, if it existed at all. However there is still a feeling in many places that the dramatherapist provides a service for all who sail in her.

It is essential that all patients are assessed before embarking on a course of dramatherapy. We may not necessarily do the assessment ourselves if we work in a multi-professional team, but we need in any case to have been consulted and be able to give second opinions if we feel there has been an error of judgement. If we are assessing ourselves, we need to have seen people individually at least once (preferably twice) and in a group several times before any recommendations are made.

The assessment is not only of whether a person can make use of dramatherapy at this particular stage in their treatment, but if so, of what model of group is most appropriate. On the following pages is a description of events from the point of referral to the actual planning of programme with decisions and their rationale.

_____ *Regional Health Authority*

MEMO:

Mr Jones (DOB 1/3/45) is attending the day centre two days a week after his discharge from hospital where he was treated for severe depression. He is a fairly isolated person and some drama work might help him to gain confidence.

First reaction:	Drama work to gain confidence? No mention of dramatherapy. Do I take this personally? (See Chapter Seven). A depressed middle aged man who is isolated.
Thinking through:	Information is minimal; no family history, class or culture; medication? Class and cultural background can influence a person's attitude towards drama; what therapeutic programme is he already part of?

We need to establish relevant family history, medical history, current therapeutic intervention AND possible reactions to the idea of drama.

Dramatherapy has an additional responsibility in its implementation since there are many assumptions by both referrers and consumers as to its nature (silly, extrovert, role-playing, 'dramatic').

More information needed:	Available family history and treatment record; current treatment including medication; pre-disposition towards drama.
More information:	After consultation with other staff and examination of records it transpires that Mr Jones was hospitalised for two months after his brother discovered that he had stayed in his room for several weeks. This followed shortly after the death of their mother with whom Mr Jones lived. He worked in the local library and was described as quiet, meticulous about his job and his person. He had been to university but left before taking his finals.
	He was now living in the family house again, attending the day centre and going to the library two mornings a week. Medication: Amitriptyline 25 mgms 3 x daily; Lithium 400 mgms a day.
	He is attending an outpatient psychotherapy group and activities at the day centre.
What more do I need to know?	What activities is he already involved in? Will what I do complement what he is already undertaking? With that medication, how much agitation leading to possible manic episodes is possible?
More information:	Further inquiry yields the following information. After the funeral Mr Jones became more and more anxious and obsessive, staying late at work to check and re-check work that he had already done; not taking lunch hours.
Further thinking through:	Mr Jones is educated and literate and used to a structured life-style. I can imagine him feeling more comfortable with reading a play and discussing it than using improvisation. I will have to be careful that any drama work does not overstimulate and make him more agitated (see below). Therefore dramatherapy that focusses on re-learning: possibly life and social skills? Communication skills? What about the death of his mother?
More information:	I ascertain that Mr Jones is attending a regular psychotherapy group twice a week run by a group psychotherapist. He is also in the social skills programme run by the occupational therapists which includes communications skills, role-play and visits outside where the skills are tested out. Patients are

also given tasks to practice at home. He attends the cooking and homecare activity groups and the large group meeting for the whole centre.

Further thinking through: The psychotherapy group is providing the place for intra-psychic change, and direct working through past traumas; and the social skills programme is already underway. I re-read the original memo and wonder whether it is exactly right: some drama work to help Mr Jones gain confidence. I make an appointment to see Mr Jones for assessment.

Assessment meeting: Mr Jones knows me by sight from the meetings and I say that it has been suggested he joins one of the dramatherapy groups. The purpose of the interview is to discuss whether we both think it a good idea. I add that there will be time to think about it and then have another meeting. He looks very guarded and says that acting is not really his scene (!). I ask him if he enjoys going to the theatre and he then describes how he took his mother regularly to see classical plays. He adds that in his work at the library he enjoys looking after the theatre and drama section, having studied literature at university. He looks guarded again when I suggest that he already knows a lot about drama, but relaxes when I say that he could perhaps make suggestions regarding the scripts we use. 'Brecht of course, and Beckett!' he says, and then proceeds to describe productions he has seen of *Mother Courage, Coriolan* and *Waiting for Godot*. I again say that this is all the dramatherapy group is about and then he voices his anxiety about having to get up and 'perform'. I reassure him that this is not the main aim of the group unless the whole group decide on a performance and then he could direct, prompt or take on other non-acting roles. I add that all the group members take part in the movement and voice sessions to both help them relax physically as well as develop their vocal strength. We end by agreeing to think things over and discuss them again.

My observations: Mr Jones is tense physically. He is a solid man of about 5' 10" and tends to sit with his hands on his lap. When he appears to get anxious he presses his hands together and clasps and unclasps them. I try sitting in his posture and my neck and shoulders start aching. I wonder about his unexpressed anger and note to discuss this in a staff meeting. He is obviously very knowledgeable about theatre and literature but very anxious about moving about. I decide to ask him about sport and gymnastics at our next interview. Structured movement and voice work feel an appropriate way forward and being able to develop his interest in the theatre. I note to pursue the following:

(a) is he doing any relaxation exercises?
(b) are any theatre visits planned?
(c) discuss what I feel to be his latent anger.

Preliminary plan: Mr Jones should join the slow open dramatherapy group where the focus is on creative expressive work. New members are able to attend for four sessions before deciding to stay. It meets once a week for two hours, with a membership of eight to twelve people.

More information: It turns out that Mr Jones is not doing any physical work or movement. The team suggest that he might be able to join the gardening group. I wonder about his capacity to tolerate mess. A theatre visit is planned and I suggest that Mr Jones is asked to help with them planning of that. The only time when any of the staff had seen him angry was when his sponge cake turned out disastrously in the cooking group and would not rise. The staff agree that my preliminary plan seems appropriate.

Second assessment meeting: Mr Jones arrives looking more wary than before and says that he does not think that drama is for him. I asked him whether he did any drama at school and he says that he was in the school play and then looked a little embarrassed. He said under his breath that he had to play Nancy in the production of *Oliver*. He had been very teased and bullied after that, and of course, called Nancy-boy. Then he looked straight at me and said 'But I enjoyed playing that role'. I said that he obviously did enjoy acting and perhaps he should give himself another chance to enjoy being in a drama. We explored the fact that he would have some autonomy in what he would and would not do, and that if he was not happy in the group then he need not stay after four weeks. He decided to try it out, but there was obviously a question mark for him. I told him that the occupational theatre staff were planning a theatre outing and would ask for his help with that. I explained to him the contract of the dramatherapy group which would also be re-iterated at the group meeting which is:

— people are not physically hurt
— verbal abuse is only allowed 'in role'
— props and furniture are not damaged.

Further thoughts: There is obviously a theme of violence and sexuality (homosexuality?) running through this man's life. The drama sessions must take into account that certain themes must trigger deeply buried material. Therefore carefully structured drama work is called for, which builds on a person's resources rather than focussing on 'problem areas'. I wonder what play he might choose if he was given the chance. I would want to keep off Edward Bond, for example, where the violence is expressed in a very direct way. He needs work that can be understood with his intellect. My guess is that anything unstructured or *seeming unstructured* could be very frightening and he could well feel that his emotions might get out of control. What do I feel about it? A little anxious, but well supported by the rest of his programme. What if? But then there is always that question with the drama.

What happened next? Mr Jones attended the first four sessions of the group. In the first sessions he attended he asked if he could just sit and watch and the group said that was fine. One of the group said to him 'Why don't you wear a tracksuit next time? You'll feel more comfortable'. He said that he didn't have one, and then a group member said that he could be allocated one if he wanted. The group were working on themes from *Five Finger Exercise* by Peter Shaffer. One of them suddenly said, 'I think Michael could play the part of Stanley.' Mr Jones looked aghast and the group member said, 'He looks the part'. I suggest that Mr Jones read the play (I am thankful that it isn't *Equus*) and that we discuss it next week.

Postscript: Subsequently Michael Jones did participate in the dramatherapy group more and more fully. He did not take the part of Stanley straight away but wanted to contribute to discussions about the play... After we had read it through we took various themes from scenes and developed them through improvisation. He did try a scene playing Stanley when it came to the point of working with families of the characters and we speculated on what family Stanley came from. The group thought that he struggled with his working class origins and being married to Louise. In role Michael Jones was able to articulate feelings of frustration and anger with his family.

STANLEY [*to* CLIVE]: And that's what you call great music? Is that right? Great music?

CLIVE [*with an attempt at humour*]: Let's say it's a little distorted at the moment.

STANLEY: Distorted? It's driving me mad.

CLIVE [*unhappily*]: I suppose we can't expect her to be an expert in two months. Run-before-you-walk Department.

LOUISE [*rises and picks up tray from coffee table. Starts to the kitchen*]: Your father imagines that everything can be done without hard work. Everything except making money out of the furniture business.

  [WALTER *re-enters from the hall and goes into his room, where he turns on the lights*]

  [*to* STANLEY] Really you are absurd. How do you think Paderewski sounded when he was practising? What is that piece she's learning, dear? Mozart? [*He shrugs, embarrassed*] Jou-Jou, I'm talking to you.

CLIVE [*low*]: Bach.

LOUISE: You could play too if you wanted to. You've got the hands for it.

  [LOUISE *goes out to the kitchen.* CLIVE *smiles faintly. There is a pause*]

STANLEY [*carefully*]: Clive, do you remember coming to the factory for your allowance the day you went up to Cambridge?

CLIVE: Yes, I do.

STANLEY: Did you have a talk to my manager while you were waiting?

CLIVE: Did I...I suppose I did.

STANLEY: Is it true you told him you thought the furniture we make was - what was it - 'shoddy and vulgar'? [*Pause*] Well?

CLIVE: I think I said it - it lacked...

STANLEY: What?

CLIVE: Well, that it didn't use material as well as it might. Wood, for example. [*He smiles hopefully*]

STANLEY: And the design was shoddy and vulgar?

CLIVE: Well, yes, I suppose I gave that impression. Not all of it, of course - just some things...

STANLEY: What things?

CLIVE [*plucking up a little courage*]: Well, those terrible oak cupboards, for example. I think you call it the Jacobean line. And those three piece suites in mauve plush. Things like that...

STANLEY [*impassive as ever*]: Mr Clark said you called them 'grotesque'.

[CLIVE *lowers his eyes*]

Is that right, grotesque?

CLIVE [*rises, crosses to commode for book, takes it to chair right of dining table*]: I think they are, rather.

STANLEY: And I suppose you think that's clever. That's being educated, I suppose; to go up to my manager

[LOUISE *enters*]

in my own factory and tell him you think the stuff I'm turning out is shoddy and vulgar....Is it?

LOUISE [*crossing to the sofa*]: Just because *you've* got no taste, it doesn't mean we all have to follow suit.

[STANLEY *gives her a look which silences her, then turns again to his son.* CLIVE *continues to sit rigid at the table*]

STANLEY: Now you listen to me, my boy. You get this through your head once and for all; I'm in a business to make money. I give people what they want. I mean ordinary people. Maybe they haven't got such wonderful taste as you and your mother; perhaps they don't read such good books - what is it? - *Homes and Gardens*? - but they know what they want. If they didn't want it, they wouldn't buy it, and I'd be out of business.

[*Piano stops*]

Before you start sneering again, young man, just remember something - you've always had enough to eat.

Peter Shaffer: Five Finger Exercise, I.ii

Comments

In talking through this piece of preliminary work before embarking upon a dramatherapy programme we can get some idea of the several factors to be taken into consideration before making any decisions. These can be summarised as follows:

— the person's history (and possible starting point for drama).
— current therapeutic programme (and how can dramatherapy complement it).
— the person's attitudes towards drama (and whether that will colour how they might use a group).

As we see from the above example, Michael Jones is already attending various groups, both activity groups and therapeutic groups. It is important that the dramatherapy does not compete with this programme but can explore other areas and also reinforce what is being undertaken. It is clear that his previous experience in the school drama had been very destructive for him as a result of the subsequent bullying. The underlying themes are appropriate material for the psychotherapy group which is a closed group and meets twice weekly. Tasks and skills are being learned and tried out within the occupational therapy programme. At this point the dramatherapist needs to ask - is it appropriate for this person to attend dramatherapy? What can I add to what is already taking place?

The thinking through that took place resulted in the following informed decision: yes, dramatherapy can provide a secure structure within which themes can be explored and articulated *through the role*; the voice and movement work can help build up the confidence and feed into the social skills work; dramatherapy itself necessitates some degree of social skill (as we have stated before), since people have to work together for it to come into being. Michael Jones had some positive experience of theatre despite the school experience and was literate in plays.

Nevertheless, choice of material needs to be careful in view of my own hunch that he could be very violent. Plays and themes that can allow for a slow expansion of inner roles seems appropriate.

Cautions

Medication: when a person is coming out of depression and is in a mid-way point between depression and anxiety, it is easy to mistake them for well. This can be particularly damaging in a dramatherapy group if too much stimulus is placed on a person, or too much pressure - even playing the part of someone who is very pressured. This stage I refer to within the dramatherapy as 'mid-point containment' which needs very careful structuring. It is a delicate balance which can allow some movement either way, ie. feeling down or feeling up, but which, through the structure, stops a final swing in either direction.

At the beginning of the 'manic phase' a person is often extremely creative - increased energy, ideas, bright eyed. This is particularly misleading to the uninitiated dramatherapist who will try to make use of this energy, interpreting it as ordinary creativity rather than understanding it within the cycle of the mood swing.[2]

Assessment

We may also use sculpting with objects or pictures, story telling and enactment within a diagnostic session. The BASICPh assessment designed by Lahad (1990)[3] is a useful procedure for looking at where the strengths are in individuals and groups and thereby the vulnerabilities.

The LIFER schema is a simplified variation on Lahad, which I use in dramatherapy diagnostic groups for ascertaining the degree of creative potential and flexibility. Like BASICPh it looks at strengths as well as weaknesses - LIFER is a guide only and not a statistically viable test.

I only use LIFER when a group has been habituated to some skills in dramatherapy in the first two diagnostic sessions and is ready for some simple improvisation in the third. I take two contrasting themes in improvisation and work with them in the group, one at a time; people work in small groups and share their mini-performance with the others. When everyone has given their presentation I get the group themselves to rate themselves and also the other group. The rating is done on the drama, the characters, scenario and content, rather than on the individuals themselves.

Lifer Chart

	low	medium	high
logic			
imagination			
feelings			
ethics			
relationship			

The purpose is to rate the piece of drama as a whole and also the characters within it, under these headings. Hence a group might have decided that, yes, their drama is very high in logic, strong in ethics, and medium in imagination, but no feelings were expressed and everyone was very isolated.

Then they repeat it for the characters in consultation with their group, so it is a collective impression and not just an individual one. They can then do it for one other small group - thus everyone has feedback as a group from one other group, self-feedback from their own group and individual feedback that has been discussed in their own group.

The dramatherapist also rates the individuals and groups and joins in the feed-back. All the assessments provide a useful guideline for the dramatherapist when making selection. It is useful to observe people's perceptions of others as well as their self-perceptions.

For example, in one improvisation on a *who dunnit* theme, the group presented a short scene from a Victorian style melodrama with heroines tied to railway track, etc - one man decided that he was the train that stopped just in time. One member of his group said:

> 'That's ridiculous playing a train - you can't do that - you
> could have been the engine driver.'

I had to give serious thought as to whether the woman would be suitable for a creative dramatherapy group - perhaps she could benefit from a structured drama games group or a more conventional performance orientated group. I would not only rely on this but make sure I provided other ways for her to explore her creative potential. When in her individual assessment she said that all her creativity had been beaten out of her (she had played the heroine on the line), her responses in the LIFER group began to make more sense.

I nevertheless felt that it would take time for her to work in a creative group and suggested that she should gain confidence in a social skills group and attend the short term assessment group as a way of building up her own creative resources.

What qualities are we looking for? I have mentioned in passing in earlier chapters the following:

- willingness to take risks with self and ideas,
- generosity of spirit in relation to others' creativity,
- potential to use the imagination.

To those I would add:

— some capacity to distinguish between reality and fantasy (see also Chapter Six on special needs),

— motivation to change, to see things from a new perspective.

However, it is an indication of these characteristics I would look for. The above listed could be the proposed outcome of the dramatherapy itself.

I would take particular care with those who are

— very hyperactive

— have psychopathic personalities

— are so depressed that suicide is a real risk.

In groups within institutions consideration needs to be given to:

— is dramatherapy the main mode of intervention?

— is it part of a range of therapeutic interventions?

If so, how does it complement the others?

— is it focussing on healthy development or is it problem orientated?

— is it part of short/medium or long term intervention?

In community settings or private practice consideration needs to be given to:

— support systems for the client in between sessions,

— relationship between therapeutic change and the domestic life setting of the individual concerned,

— clinical monitoring in addition to supervision,

— back-up support for crisis intervention.

Aims and objectives are clearly understood, eg, that therapy is not undertaken in a situation that purports to be an evening class.

The reader should also consider the codes of ethics and practice for dramatherapists.

The ritual-risk paradigm

Every dramatherapy session has a component of ritual and risk, and the balance of these two elements varies with the particular client group and may vary over time as people change and develop.

The ritual factor creates the safety, the predictable, the known. It may be the map we look at before we start a journey. It may be the movement, chants or song that the group creates to start and end; it is a statement which acts as a container for change, for the journey, for the adventure.

The risk factor is the unexpected, it catches us unawares, it is the unknown journey and can take us into uncharted territory, it can result from a particular theme or can spontaneously arise - it can even be totally unexpected for the dramatherapist (which is where the internal supervisor and creative artist need to be very much in evidence). It is impossible to prescribe this balance totally, though the following are useful guidelines:

People whose lives are high risk anyway, or who are hyper-stimulated/hyperactive, need more ritual than risk and may need an all-ritual group to create new frames of being. Too much risk is likely to blow the fuse and become destructive for client and therapist alike. People who live low risk lives, are highly institutionalised or functioning well below their possible potential, need less ritual and more risk factor. However, all groups need the basic ritual security that establishes the working security and framework for the group.

I described in Chapter One the basic developmental paradigm of *embodiment, projection, role*; this, taken in conjunction with the ritual risk paradigm, is a very basic dramatherapy starting point for intervention.

If in doubt, start with embodiment; not only is it developmentally sound, it is also where the majority of people need to start. Most people who come to dramatherapy groups need to work on their body-self and change in self image, they need to find ways of creating with their own body, including their voices; the body becomes a creative instrument through which they can re-discover trust and strength and extend their own experience of life into other worlds.

With people for whom body work is too threatening, I usually start with projective work using sculpting, pictures, puppets. Through toys, dolls and objects, we can create small scenarios of stories and life happenings. They can be more manageable when they exist in miniature form so that people can be on the outside and look in, and venture to the inside as they become more adventurous (see Jennings 1986 for a range of dramatherapeutic methods and a description of their application).

Role work usually comes much later in a group, once people have become more comfortable with body and voice work. It may lead on from sculpting using people rather than toys, it may stem from text - from a two line vignette - or it can be the core of a story for which people improvise several endings. I hesitate to use the term 'role play', as so many clients have fearful associations of being made to look silly, of not knowing what to say. I find the term enactment, or dramatisation is less threatening and one that can progressively be introduced into movement and voice work.

Always, take a pulse on the groups and individual presence and rely both on the internal therapist and the internal artist to guide you. Since all people are creative by their very nature, it is not that dramatherapy is not suitable but that we have not found the best place to start.

> 'Chaplin, Caruso, Sid Field, Edith Evans, Spike Milligan, Peter Sellers, Louis Armstrong, John Gielgud, the Carolis, Johnny Puleo, the Fratellinis, Ellen Terry, Larry Olivier, Robert Donat, Paul Scofield, Dan Leno, Beatrice Lillie, Wences, Edwige Feuillere, Flagstad, Eva Turner, Jean Louis Barrault, Harry Secombe - the list could go on forever - all doctors, nurses and psychiatrists in their own humble or arrogant way, transporting us into worlds beyond our everyday selves, either by escape from reality (and what harm in that?) or by escape into a deeper reality, either by helping us to forget or, if we can bear it, to remember.'
>
> *Miles and Trewin: Curtain Calls, p 11*

Chapter Four

Dramatherapy with Groups

'I saw more than I can tell and understood more than I saw'

Neihardt, Black Elk Speaks, p 43

Imagine a family in their sitting room. A man is sitting behind a newspaper, we can see his legs and the top of his head; a woman is sitting at a table writing a letter. There are three children; two are playing in a corner and the third is reading a book. An old woman is sitting in a wheel chair, looking into the distance, her hands rest on the rug which covers her legs.

The scene is 'frozen' for a moment so that we can do some appraisal. What else do we need to know before we make an intervention?

1. *Where* is this scene taking place?

We already know that it is in the sitting room but whose sitting room? What kind of house is this room in? How many rooms? Do these people live there? All of them? Is this a town or country house? In the UK, Europe, Eastern Bloc? Does anything in this space give us a sense of where?

2. *When* is this scene taking place?

There is little from the above description that we might assume although we could probably guess that it is daytime since the old woman and children are still up - unless of course it is a special celebration. What season is it? What year in which century? Which day of the week and what time of day? How can we tell if this is an everyday time for these people or a special time?

3. *Who* are all these people?

We are told it is a family. Are we to assume that the three children are from the same parents? Are the man and woman married to each other? Have they been married once? Whose mother/aunt is the old lady?

Family Picture

4. *Why* are these people in this room together?

Maybe this is a typical family gathering. Or is it grandma's visiting day and they have just had lunch? Are they celebrating? Decision making? Or is this another bored non-communicative scene where everything is unsaid?

5. *What* is this scene about?

Perhaps is shows the normality of this family. Or is there a key factor that we do not yet know? Is there a person missing? Is anyone actually saying anything out loud or are all the conversations silent ones?

I want you to imagine that this is a dramatherapy 'sculpt'; try it with some colleagues or friends and see how many scenarios are possible.

This is called the Where, When, Who, What, Why[1] exercise and is useful, not only in training groups but in approaching all the groups we may work with. It guards us against making assumptions about what we see. And what about anything that escaped our attention, that we did not see? What grabbed our attention first? Did it literally jump out at us? Is that significant for the people in the scene or does it belong to similar images in our own lives? (see Chapter Seven: therapist's own resources).

The process that we are engaged with is both *expanding* the frame of the scene (like using a wide-angle lens) and *focussing* the element(s) (like using a zoom lens). It is the process of the dramatic imagination which both expands and focusses the scenario. It is a process that we continually need to practice in order to develop our own imagination.

For example, in relation to the above scene, the expansion results in an awareness of what we term *worlds within worlds*; i.e. the room within the house within the street within the community within the district within the region within the country within the continent within the world (location in space). It also gave us an understanding of the moment within the hour within the day within the week within the month within the year within the decade within the century (location in time). The people in the picture represent individuals within a family within three generations within a network within a population (location in personae). The *where, when* and *who* sets the scene for any piece of drama whether it is a play or therapy.

If we now look at the picture of the above scene, we may, for example be aware of the man, probably the father, reading the newspaper; why is he reading *Le Monde* and holding it in front of his face? Does he not want to be seen or is this what he wants us to see? If we see this then what are we not seeing? We then notice that he is wearing gloves; is it cold or does he not want us to see his hands? Why is the woman writing a letter? Is she writing to her lover hoping to escape from this scene? Or is it a letter to her mother who lives abroad, telling her how difficult it is in a strange country coping with her husband's extended family? Or is it a letter to the local authority which states her mother must go into a home? The focus helps us 'get inside' the specifics of these people in this place at this time. The *why* and the *what* uncovers the many layers from generality to specificity; they fine-tune the characters in the drama.

The expansion and the focus of the scene are the particular properties of the drama which are engaged through the dramatic imagination. This process enables an awareness of the multi-dimensional nature of the dramatic presentation.

The scene with which I commenced this chapter is in fact a photograph of a family taken in 1944; a Franco-Polish emigré family who escaped to the UK during the Nazi occupation. The photo was taken by the father's brother to accompany the letter that mother is writing to her father who is in hospital in France. The scene is in the sitting/living room of a small apartment where this family live: mother, father and their two children; father's brother and his child; and the widowed mother of the two brothers. Father is an invalid and is badly scarred, his mother is deaf, mother 'copes', the two children, twins, create their own world, their cousin usually plays apart and misses his own mother, and uncle tries very hard to be the able man of the household. The entire family is depressed and burdened.

The photograph is one of many that I use in direct work both with trainees and clients. With trainees, I may ask them to reconstruct the picture in terms of a living family with a history, environment and dynamics. The training group is divided into smaller groups and each group is given the same photograph. After they have spent some time re-creating the family, they are asked to present either a scene from the family's past, (where has it come from? or how did it get here?) or to bring the present scene alive by dramatising it. They explore what they have learned about the characters and the relationships by becoming the scene rather than only talking about it. One group felt very strongly that the grandfather clock was important and created a character for the clock as the container of the family history (see also the Brown family drama where they use *environmental objects*, p 91) Having presented the scene, the trainees then suggest possible therapeutic interventions, try them out and get feed-back from the characters. I shall discuss this approach of *living drama* as contrasted with *role-play* later in this chapter.

Alternatively, I describe the scenario of the photograph and ask the group to dramatise a scene from the family's past or future. We can use the photograph and description as if it is a case history, and let part of the group dramatise the characters. The others, in pairs, can interview the family, make an assessment, experiment with therapeutic intervention. The possibilities and learning are endless with this one picture and the learning is endless.

When I am working with clients, I rarely use the actual story, though it is interesting how many people get near to the facts of the story through enacting the characters and scenes. One way of commencing family work with groups (as well as a family *in situ*) is to start with a stimulus such as a picture, photograph or story. This helps to make the bridge into the dramatic convention. That is, instead of creating a dramatisation of the client's actual family, he or she is asked to choose a picture. Usually the choice is quite conscious, eg, 'I am choosing this picture because my granny sits in a chair' or 'my dad always hides behind the newspaper'. It is usually a visible association that guides a person's choice. Inevitably there are unconscious connections that the person makes that become manifest in the dramatisation. I reinforce the bridge into the dramatic convention by keeping the focus on the picture, rather than the person's own situation. The group as a whole is invited to contribute and comment on the picture and its content, and I suggest that we create a story to enact from the picture. Group members choose roles, set the scene - as it is in the photo if they are working in the present, or make suggestions if it is from the past. The dramatisation tells the story of the picture and the picture may be the beginning of the story or the end. The group may divide into smaller groups to work at their own ending for the story and the several endings are contrasted. Everyone finds something of their own story within the picture and through the dramatisation discovers the possibility of movement and change. It is important to stay with the picture and then the drama, than to refer back to peoples' own lives. As I described in Chapter One, the dramatic metaphor creates the distance in order for exploration to take place at a deeper level.

The following is an account of an exploration of this picture with a client group of men and women aged between 20 and 50 years who have been referred for dramatherapy for various degrees of distress in their lives.

Personae

Mary: 38 years, single, worked part-time as a teacher and looked after a bedridden mother.

Diana: 22 years, stabilised anorectic, still pre-occupied with food, studying at a polytechnic.

Joan: 45 years, divorced, lonely, fighting for survival.

Naomi: 30 years, overweight, desperate to have a baby, on the verge of marriage break-up.

Chris: 27 years, tense, frightened, obsessive about his work as a clerk.

John: 25 years, always tired, dropped out of college, talented musician but too tired to practice.

Lenny: 41 years, wants to change his life but feels it's too late, burdened by weight of family and finance.

The group meets weekly for two hours and has been together for three months. The early life of the group has focussed on *developing the skills for articulation* - body and voice - and using them to explore a range of emotions within various roles. The group chose roles from fairy-stories they remembered and attached emotions to them such as jealous step-mother, angry father, sad princess. They then chose a fairy story - *Little Red Riding Hood* - to dramatise, which led into some exploration of different themes about forests (see Chapters Four and Five). The journeys into the forest resulted in someone saying, 'I want to go indoors now'.

(The reader is invited to free-associate all the possible themes that this statement brings to mind.)

Session 14

Warm-up

I show the group a collection of 'indoor' pictures which includes doors, windows, interiors with and without people, a cage with a gorilla inside and so on and I suggest that we choose one picture to work with. There is some deliberation while the pictures are passed round, and phrases such as:

'I want to break out of my cage', 'the empty room, who might be there?', 'knock three times and I'll tell you your fortune', 'Why don't we do a "who dunnit" and I'll be the murderer'. *Mary* says that she wants to work with the picture described above, saying, 'The old lady in the chair, I know what that's about'. *Lenny* says, 'what is it about?' and *Naomi* says, 'Don't ask direct questions'.

Intervention: 'I wonder what the picture is about?' *Everyone studies their copy assiduously, and people look at it closely, holding it at a distance.*

Where?

Well, it's a house - the living room; the furniture is old;
maybe it's a country house - with ghosts;
no, it's in London, Victorian, in a square;
I bet Sherlock Holmes goes there - there's a mystery;
Maybe it's not in England, maybe they're English abroad;

or foreigners in England;
it must be in England - look at the clock and the windows;

When?

I still say it's Victorian - look at the clothes and the HAIR;
no, they're just poor people;
poor, what about the clock?
the clock says six o'clock and it's not in the bloody morning;
so it's evening - and it's winter;
why?
he's wearing gloves - and the blanket;
I bet there's a coal fire;

Who?

It's a family - mother, father, children and grandma;
how do you know it's her husband?
maybe he and the old woman are ill and she's looking
after them;
he's hiding - is he a criminal?
course he is with those gloves on;
no-one looks happy;
they are all turned away - no-one looks at each other;
it's a trap - they can't escape;

Intervention:

who took the photograph? grandad; teenage son; uncle;
maid; policeman;

Why?

they're waiting for something;
no - it's always like that - I know what *no-speak* families
are like;
children being ignored - no-one is doing anything for them;
what do you mean - *no-speak*?
nobody ever speaks - they just give orders or criticise;
they've just had tea - having a rest;
they're bored;
they're going to be taken away and shot;
the French Revolution;

What?

        she's going to put her in a home;
        she's writing her secret diary;
        it's a letter of complaint to the nursing home;
        no - it says she can't cope;
        she's a nurse and she's writing a report;
        they've had a bust-up and no-one is speaking;
        they never speak;
        he's going to strangle the old lady, that's why he is
        wearing gloves;
        this scene is about a family that does not communicate.
        so the photographer is the therapist?

Intervention: If this family went to therapy, what would it be about?
        What would be said?

Mary: What isn't being said you mean.
Diana: The children must speak.

A hubbub ensues of who needs to speak to who about what; voices are raised.

Intervention: I suggest that everyone chooses a character. The following
        are immediately chosen.

Mary: The woman, and I'm getting some poison, *she adds.*
Diana: The small child reading.
Joan: The woman, and I'm nice and caring.
Naomi: The old woman - just like I feel.
Chris: The man.
John: I want to be the photographer, and I'm a neighbour.
Lenny: I want to be the old woman but can I be an old man?

The group agrees that he can; then *John* says that he'd like to be a child if someone else will be;

Intervention: Everyone can play several roles.

Mary suddenly says that she would like to play a child.

(*Teaching point*: the therapist needs to gauge the balance between the free-float-ing exploration as above and the introduction of dramatic structure. This group has high energy and it needs some focus before it is dissipated. Notice how the group keep within the dramatic reality).

Intervention: Are we working in the present or the past of this picture?

John says that we should work with the time before the woman became a widow, before her husband died.

I use the flip chart to keep track of these relationships and draw the following under their direction:

First scenario

grandpa = grandma

|

daughter = husband

b. twins g.   g.

Diana:	And the dad has an accident - and the baby is not his 'cos the mother had an affair.
Chris:	With his brother!
Chorus:	The photographer.
Lenny:	It's the grandparents' house, that's the tension.
Chris:	So the kids have to behave; you know what old people are like.

Intervention: I suggest that to start with, one group works on adult characters and another group works on child characters.

Joan, Naomi, Chris and *Lenny* choose to be adults.

Diana, Mary and *John* choose to be children.

They move into to their two groups and we agree they have five minutes for talk-ing and then they begin to improvise the characters and create a scene.

(*Teaching point*: The group are familiar with working in this way and I move from group to group, side coaching where necessary.)

The two groups move into separate spaces and discuss their characters and the scene they want to portray. The 'adults' stay on their chairs and the 'children' decide to sit on the floor.

The adult group want to present a scene when the daughter and her parents are discussing her marriage; they want her to marry Captain Phipps - with prospects - she wants to marry Jimmy, a sailor who plays the flute - Captain Phipps' brother.

They work at a confrontation between the parents and the daughter - mother is very strong - dad follows what she says - he's weak but does not question what his wife says - daughter hasn't got an ally - only child - mother talks about prospects - security - daughter talks about love and friendship - Captain plays up to parents - smarmy devil - he does what they want - (*Chris* asks if he can play both the Captain and Jimmy and his group agree) - they want to play the scene between Jimmy and the daughter.[3]

Intervention:	Can we continue the scene next week and right now think of a key sentence for each character.

Mother:	You'll thank me in years to come.
Father:	Your mother is quite right.
Daughter:	Jimmy is very trustworthy - and he really loves me.
Capt. Phipps:	I have your daughter's interest at heart.
Jimmy:	I will take you on the journey of your dreams.

The group presents a short scene between the parents and the daughter and then the arrival of the Captain.

Intervention:	Stay in character and create a sculpt of the relationship between the parents and daughter.

The mother stands with one hand on the daughter's shoulder and the other hand gesturing out in a grand sweep - the father puts one hand round his wife's waist and the other on his daughter's shoulder - the daughter stands with both shoulders weighed down - one foot pointing away and one towards her parents - her face looks over her other shoulder.

They say their key sentences.

(*Teaching point*: There is already a lot of material being expressed through the characters and the temptation is to move too fast - for example, the sculpt illustrates the sub-text of this scene rather than the key sentences - so it is important for the therapist to pace the session.)

The other group decides to play a scene when the youngest was a baby - she lies on a cushion and makes baby noises - the twin girl says to the twin boy - 'Ssh, Mummy says we must be quiet.'

He says:	Why can't we play like we used to?
She says:	Let's play when she was born - she's so weak she dies.
He says:	I'll be the doctor and bring the baby.
She says:	Dead.

Intervention:	Again, can we explore further scenes next week and now think of the key sentences.

Twin boy:	Why won't dad play?
Twin girl:	I didn't want a sister - specially a favourite one
Baby:	Please let me play - I didn't want to be the favourite.

(*Teaching point*: We are still working within the drama through character, dialogue, embodiment and sculpting; any discussion is within the character - for example, when *Diana* says, 'I feel so split,' my reply is, 'As the daughter, you feel very split.')

Intervention:	We have 55 minutes left of this session, lets explore the characters further through a character analysis and then we'll have time for a wind-down - we can continue with these scenes next week.

(*Teaching point*: For the character analysis, everyone writes about their character in the first person and includes any information that comes spontaneously to mind; there is side coaching which feeds in ideas such as - what did you eat for breakfast - what are your beliefs, stated or secret? I give the group a maximum of ten minutes.)[4]

The following is *Lenny's* character analysis as the father in the 'adult's' scene:

> 'My name is George and I am 55 years old, I love my
> daughter and my wife but I don't often say much - my
> wife is a good woman but I am sometimes scared of her -
> she looks after us well - sometimes she is a bit fierce with
> our only daughter - I don't want my daughter to leave
> home and if she marries the Captain then we'll see more of
> her - I like a quiet life and am not very adventurous - bit

like my own Dad - I work hard to provide for the family
and we have a nice house - I feel a lot of pressure to keep
up the standards my wife expects - I'm quite a simple man
really - simple tastes in food and clothes - quiet drink with
my friends - secretly I envy my daughter and her chance
of romance, though I'd never dare admit it to her mother -
this Jimmy fellow is easy going and relaxed and does silly
things my daughter loves - like scattering daffodils all over
her car - but my wife is very puritanical - and nothing
must be a mess - but I do like my routine - I buy the *Times*
everyday and I always watch Panorama - Sundays are
good days when I play golf and have a roast Sunday lunch
- maybe there is a God but I don't challenge him - now my
wife is certain God exists - part of life's pattern.'

The group all read out their character analyses, listening intently to each other.

The groups start to discuss whether they agree with what people have said and I point out that what people have written is to be accepted, even if others have a different perception. *Chris* says that people often make judgements which are not what a person really feels, 'nobody knows who I really am' he blurts out and tears come into his eyes. This becomes a key theme for the whole group and I suggest that each person makes a personal statement about assumptions.

(*Teaching point*: This is the beginning of the transition from the character to peoples' own lives; it is part of the de-roling and distancing process already described.)

Mary:	I've always had to be the 'nice' person - a woman who looks after people.
Diana:	Me too; Daddy's little girlie.
Joan:	And me! I was never allowed any opinions of my own.
Naomi:	I want to be a woman - and a mother - nobody takes me seriously.
Chris:	You've a good brain - do something sensible with it.
John:	Being unconventional will only get you into trouble and music isn't a manly occupation.
Lenny:	You're such a responsible person and you'll make some woman very happy.

Intervention: We have 20 minutes left before the group closes; let's
                         share anything we want to say about the characters and
                         the scenes.

What a family - it's so depressed - there's something with the father - there are
secrets in this family - the daughter obviously marries the captain - maybe she still
loves the brother - I liked being a child and wanting my sister dead - I wish I was
dead - you mean in the play? - well - maybe - I think the old woman's husband died
of a heart attack - I don't know that he's dead - maybe he's in hospital - I think the
old woman is still strong even though she is old - too true - maybe Jimmy will come
and rescue everyone - I wanted to play with my dad - not always being left with my
sister.

Intervention: Is there a particular character that you would like to explore
                         next week?

All of the men say they would like to play Jimmy, the sailor, and three of the women
want to play the daughter; Joan says she wants to play the old woman.

Intervention: It's almost time to stop - let's look at the photo again and
                         imagine it is part of a play we have just seen - that we are
                         watching it rather than being part of it.

Everyone looks again at the photo and seem surprised at what they had developed
from the image and also what they had forgotten was there.

She looks so meek - so sweet - I bet she's really angry and can't show it - the children
are older than I thought - is the old woman blind? - he's reading *Le Monde* - it's a
French newspaper - it means the world - it's our world isn't it?

Intervention: Take one last look at the photo and then close your eyes -
                         imagine that you have been seeing the play on a film -
                         the scene with the parents - the scene with the children...
                         the film comes to an end and it says on the screen - to be
                         continued next week.

                         Spend a few moments letting go of anything you are still
                         carrying of the character you have been playing and feel
                         yourself again - your age - in this room with the other people
                         in the dramatherapy group - can you remember what
                         everyone is wearing?... Visualise the room and the clock
                         on the wall which says 7.55 - listen to the tick of the clock -

finally check whether your body feels tense - breathe
deeply - and when you are ready - open your eyes.

People open their eyes and stretch - there is some laughter as people check out what
each other is wearing - Mary says, 'there's so much anger there' and Lenny agrees
with her.

They leave the room in twos and threes.

(*Teaching points*: The time taken for de-roling is very important and needs to be
structured as a gradual process. Notice how the group stays within the drama,
referring to the character - what the character feels, is doing etc. - until the last half
hour. Then through feed-back - which is not personal revelation such as 'it's just
like my mother' - but a commentary on the characters and scenes. At one level the
group know they are also talking about themselves but the dramatic paradox enables
them to say and experience far more.

A group theme emerged - of judgements being made about us - this is the only direct personal work which is structured in response to the group theme.

The photo is used again at the end to distance people from the experience - help-
ing them to see it as separate from themselves - then more time is allowed for the
re-establishing of self. The use of the photo also acts as a reductionist mechanism
- especially when people have been dealing with larger than life feelings, often
experiencing a sense of being overwhelmed, or of going out of control. The
photo reduces everything to size again, a 'pocket image' that they can put away if
they need to.)

It is human beings' capacity to move between the epic and the micro that enables
dramatherapy to work effectively on inner and outer experience. It is the task of the
dramatherapist to sense when these shifts need to be structured and when they will
occur naturally through the creative process. The dramatherapist's internal artist
needs to be ever-present.

The following is an extract from my notes after this session:

Group Notes:

On the drama

People wanted to get into script
very quickly - worked in small
intimate drama - no sense of
fourth wall?- characterisation-
authentic, through line *not*

On the group

There seems to be a common
core of suffering around spaces;
external expectations/assumptions
splits; where are the
transferences? the characters

established, though sub-text in sculpts - more embodiment is necessary maybe group sculpts?

of the parents so what hidden agendas about me? children?

Individuals:

Mary:
As child portrayal very vicious eyes flashing, hands tense.

Sudden switch from adult to child - who does she want dead?

Diana:
Authentic 'little girl';

'I wish I was dead' - has said this before; 'I wish the fat me was dead.'

Joan:
Brought a pathos to the daughter as someone trapped.

Identification with daughter? seems very lonely in group

Naomi:
Very strong as mother, vocally and physically.

Total contrast to her tearful role in the group

Chris:
Played himself it seems as the Captain - not engaged dramatically.

Big strides, much more vocal

John:
Authentic boy child (????)

Did not seem a sleepy child!

Lenny:
Brilliant characterisation as economy of voice and movement, group sense of the drama.

Burdened - expectation - the father - fear of change - too nice to the group

Personal reflections

Some anxiety about containment - familiar pain between the shoulders - holding the reigns? A host of images - Hermia's struggle in *Midsummer Night's Dream* - the two sculpts - child abuse in the children's one? intuition?

Next session
More embodiment and group sculpts - everyone to have chance to play adult and child - addressing splits - what two of me are in this scene?

The above extract is part of the notes made shortly after the session; the following are the *diary notes* made during the ensuing few days.

In the ensuing week I'm nagged by an image that won't quite surface - the more I think about it, the more elusive it becomes.

Golden rule: don't force the unconscious!

I try to switch off and make a note to take the issue to my supervision group. I am concerned that the process of this group will impinge on other work that I am doing. (These and other issues for the dramatherapist are explored fully in Chapter Seven). However I am aware of feeling heavy, the shoulder pain continues together with a feeling of something being just over the horizon - that I ought to be aware of. OUGHT? Am I stuck too in expectation? I look at the photo again and realise that I have not fully de-roled myself (an occupational hazard for dramatherapists), and in a busy week of teaching, writing and working with clients, I make a conscious decision to have time for a complete change.

I take a couple of hours off for a walk on Hampstead Heath - to scuff leaves in the autumn chill and spend time by the ponds - few people are there on a midweek afternoon and the wind bites sharply - I start to run, shouting into the wind and end up gasping for breath, leaning against a tree trunk - the pools are still with ripple movements on the surface as the wind blows in intermittent gusts - there are two or three fisherman, still and silent under their green umbrellas - I keep walking and decide to circuit the pools.

Tramp, tramp, leaves and mud - face dry from the wind - time will soon be up - the sound of voices blows across and I turn to put the hair out of my eyes - there are two children coming closer with an adult woman - the children are holding hands and approach the water - the boy is pointing out a half sunken tree in the centre of the pool - 'Look, it's a monster from the deep', he says, and his sister (I assume) opens her eyes wide and starts to suck her thumb - the adult woman, who looks bored and disinterested, shakes them both and gestures them to walk on - she walks away, frozen faced - the children stay by the pool and they hold on to each other - I'm just watching, half concealed by a tree - it feels very familiar and I'm rivetted - the children are staring at the sunken tree and the dark water lapping round the submerged trunk - there is a tangle of leaves, twigs and feathers caught up in the branches - just then a loud voice breaks the silence;

COME HERE - NOW!

The children start, look at each other, and walk meekly in the direction of the voice of their companion - the scene returns to its quietness, the wind and water cover over the little interlude that I have witnessed - I am left feeling uneasy.

I start to walk away - then the image hammers onto my brain - *The Turn of the Screw* - Henry James - that's the image that has eluded me from the group - the children - frozen - a sense of evil -

> 'I transferred my eyes straight to little Flora, who, at the moment, was about ten yards away. My heart had stood still for an instant with the wonder and terror of the question whether she too would see; and I held my breath while I waited for what a cry from her, what some sudden innocent sign either of interest or alarm, would tell me. I waited, but nothing came; then, in the first place - and there is something more dire in this, I feel, than in anything I have to relate - I was determined by a sense that within a minute all sponta- neous sounds from her had dropped; and in the second by the circumstance that also within the minute she had, in her play, turned her back to the water. This was her attitude when I at last looked at her - looked with the confirmed conviction that we were still, together, under direct personal notice. She had picked up a small flat piece of wood which happened to have in it a little hole that had evidently suggested to her the idea of sticking in another fragment that might figure as a mast and make the thing a boat.'
>
> *James: The Turn of the Screw, p 181*

I walk home with a lighter step - I don't address the image - this is my two hour break so I put it on the back-burner for future attention.

As one of my supervisees said recently:

> 'Will the day ever come when I can look at a sunset for its own sake, instead of thinking - I could use that in a dramath- erapy session?'

This time out is essential for all creative artists and therapists; its rationale is discussed more fully in Chapter Seven.

The morning of the day that the group is due to meet, I spend my usual time *thinking through* in preparation for the session. I read through the previous week's notes and ponder *The Turn of the Screw* image - children taken over by the woman (nurse? step-mother? aunt?), a sense of evil - who has abused who? There is always the dilemma - which material needs to stay buried and which needs to be explored?

I remember that the group had selected two characters that most of them wanted to explore: one character from the photo - the woman/daughter/mother; and one character that they had created - the romantic sailor-lover, Jimmy. The dramatic possibilities are endless and, as always, there is a tension between the artist and the therapist. My internal therapist focusses on the pathology of the group - stuckness - abuse (?) - splits - aspects of self that have been denied - *pacing* the change - the unsticking.

Stay with the drama - keep the structure - see where the group is - keep the range of possibilities *waiting in the wings* - the intuition that will not go away is the sculpt of the children - but it also feels too powerful to deal with it now. The group wants to explore the characters, so let's stay with that.

Session 15

The group arrives in varying form; *Mary* is irritable and impatient; *Diana* looks very pale; *Joan* looks as if she has a lot to say; *Naomi* is huffy and sulking; *Chris* is smiling; *John* looks bright with dark circles under his eyes; *Lenny* has not yet arrived.

We come together in the circle and review the intervening week; there is some chatting and speculation as to *Lenny's* whereabouts, then *Naomi* says she has had a very bad week and her mother bought her a box of chocolates to cheer up. *Diana* looks at her and goes even paler, *Mary* tells *Naomi* to shut up and stop bleating, *Chris* continues to smile and says he's bought a new tie and is wearing it for the first time. The group remark on the picture on the tie - a parrot - a plumed cockatoo with a palm tree; *John* is alert but says nothing and looks over his shoulder towards the door.

Lenny arrives ten minutes late - sorry, sorry - no I'm not - I'm glad, he says as he sits on the vacant chair. The group round on him - *glad*? *Mary* says it's bloody rude, *Lenny* says, I am late for the first time to the group - to work - and to home - so there!

Some bickering ensues and my hunch is that people are postponing the start of the group. Whenever I introduce the theme, somebody starts another quibble, so I suggest that we make two groups - one concerned with the rules of the group and one less bothered by the rules.

Mary, Naomi, Diana and *Chris* join together in one group for the rules. *Joan, Lenny* and *John* create the opposite group.

Intervention: Create a sculpt to illustrate the theme - rules or no rules - each group is to do both sculpts.

The group want to sit down and talk about it but I suggest they move around and warm themselves up and then experiment with the sculpts. The group is struggling, desultory and unfocussed.

Intervention: *I go into role as a regimental sergeant major*, RIGHT, attention, quick march in formation.

People pause for only a moment and then come to attention and start marching. I keep the theme going with marching backwards and forwards and so on. As we stop, people remark how easy it is to get into the idiom and follow the orders.

Intervention: Right, move into a space, shakes your bodies out, shake every muscle, feel yourself getting lighter and lighter - and you are being blown across the room, hither and thither, feel yourself very light and being carried by the wind.

The group works with the complete contrast of the movement, letting go of their tense muscles and wafting round the room, occasionally bumping into each other.

Intervention: Spread your arms out and whirl, spin and glide round the room and then come to rest in your small groups, and continue with the sculpts.

The energy has shifted in the group, it is not high energy but it is focussed and the sniping has stopped. I give the group three minutes to create the sculpts.

The first group divides into two pairs and stand as if they are doing formation dancing to represent rules; they then stand facing each other as if they were going to strip and make love.

The second group looks a little taken aback. Their first sculpt shows them standing in a row, pointing fingers, as if they were ordering children to obey. For their second sculpt they join hands as if they were dancing and singing.

Intervention: So dancing can be strict or free?

We returned to the group and people began to talk about last week. *Lenny* started by saying how he had walked away with a feeling of being lighter and also mischievous and had gone home and suggested to his wife that they went out to a night club. She had said 'no - we've never done anything like that,' and he said, 'well, will you think about it?' He had overslept and been late for work - joined some colleagues after work for a drink - been late home and his wife thought he had gone to a night club on his own - and he decided to see how it felt being late to the group - he said all this without interruption and then *Chris* smiled and said it gave him some hope since

Lenny reminded him of his dad. *Mary* said she felt like bursting out with anger and *Diana* said she felt ill; *Naomi* said nothing and *John* asked to get on with the play, and *Joan* echoed him.

Intervention: Do we need to look at the photograph again?

Generally - no - let's look at it afterwards - what are we going to do this week - I still want to play Jimmy.

Intervention: Well, last week, several people wanted to explore Jimmy and
                           several the woman in the photo - let's divide into a male and
                           female group and work with that first - five minutes
                           discussion to focus on the character.

They move into a group of men and a group of women.

I move between the two groups, feeding in ideas such as, who is Jimmy? How long has he played the flute? How does the woman make herself heard? Does she really want to leave the family? I remind the group that they can focus on the where, when, who, why and what of the characters to help them re-engage with the drama. When the five minutes is up, I ask them to create a group sculpt of each character.

The women's group

Mary and *Naomi* stand back to back; *Mary* has her hands by her sides, palms forward, with a sweet smile; *Naomi's* hands cover her face and her shoulders are bowed, *Joan* sits on the floor close to *Naomi* with her fingers like spikes, darting round her body; *Diana* lies flat on the floor with one of *Mary's* feet on her chest.

Intervention: Keep the position of the sculpt and make a statement of
                           what your part of the sculpt is saying - begin the statement
                           with I, and repeat it several times.

Mary *(sweetly):*   Of course I'm a good wife and mother, of course I'll take
                           care of you.
Naomi: I am crying enough to fill the sea.
Joan: I'm so angry, I'm full of hate and fury.
Diana *(gasping)*:   Yes, I'll do what you say.

Intervention: Say the phrase quietly and slowly, then let them get louder
                           and louder; each speak one at a time - the men will echo what

you say as a chorus, using *you* instead of I - let the phrases get louder then softer, down to a whisper.

The dramatic chorus which echoes between individuals and group is very powerful and results in an interaction between *Diana* and the chorus of men as follows:

Diana: Yes, I'll do as you say (*foot on her chest*).

Chorus: Yes, you'll do as we say.

The chorus have unconsciously adopted the sculpt of last week and are all pointing their fingers at her. *Diana* starts to struggle physically and says, 'I can't, I can't'.

Intervention: Freeze the sculpt; *to Diana* - what can't you?

Diana: I can't do as he says - I can't, I won't - I feel sick.

Intervention: Who in the sculpt can help you with this?

Joan: She needs my anger - she just can't lie there - she has to fight.

Intervention: What is the name of the woman in the scene?

She hasn't got a name - she's grey - call her anything - no - she is something like Sybil - or Claire - I think she's a Jane - definitely a Jane.
    The group seem to agree on the name and I continue:

Intervention: *Joan*, as the angry part of Jane, move closer to *Diana* as the helpless part of Jane - and both of you repeat your statements to the men's chorus.

They do this, and instead of feebly struggling, *Diana* starts to show some internal anger and changes her statement to -

                'I won't do what you say, I'm full of hate and fury.'

(*Teaching point*: The therapist has a choice here - whether to explore the specifics of *Diana's* situation which I surmise is about abuse, or whether to work from within the feelings within the drama i.e. the *living drama*. A psychodramatist would probably do the former. As a dramatherapist, all my antennae, especially my internal artist *and* supervisor, say to stay within the dramatic mode. I therefore decide to *role reverse* the sculpt.

Intervention: Freeze the sculpt; (*Diana is already half sitting and shaking her fist*), remember the position you have now and your body feeling. I am asking the men to now create the sculpt - as you dissolve the sculpt, leave the character in the space and walk away from it - chorus do the same.

They walk away from the space - shake their arms - the men complain of tension as they had pointed their fingers for so long, and *Mary* remarks that her smile is fixed - *Diana* is swinging her clenched fist around as if it is a completely new movement for her.

The men's group

The men spend a few moments deciding how they will portray the sculpt, and then take up the following positions -

Chris kneels on the floor with his head bowed. *Lenny* puts a foot on his back, and *John* holds his hands over his ears with his whole body stooping and limp - there is a sense of him cowering.

Intervention: Are the sentences the same? Say what feels appropriate - chorus, wait a moment.

Lenny: I'll take care of you - I'm strong.

Chris: I am a good child, really I am.

John: I'm afraid, I don't want to listen.

Intervention: Is there something missing in the sculpt?

Naomi: The anger - they haven't got the anger.

Chris: I am angry but I can't show it.

Intervention: Can you include that in your statement?

Chris: I'm angry and can't show it, so I'm a good child.

Intervention: Right, as the different aspects of Jane, let's set up the phrases and let the chorus respond to them. Who do we think the chorus represent for Jane?

Her father - no, her mother - both her parents - part of her self that she's got to listen to - most of all her father.

They work at the individual/chorus interaction again and as *Chris's* statements get louder, he begins to raise his head and *Lenny's* foot slips off his back. He falls off balance against *John* who snarls 'don't push me around'.

Intervention: Keep that as your line.

The interaction becomes:

Lenny: I'll look after you, I'm strong.

Chorus: You'll look after us, you're strong.

Chris: I am so angry, I can't be good.

Chorus: You are so angry, you can't be good.

John: Don't push me around.

Chorus: We'll push you around.

(*Teaching point*: It is important at this point to structure the *voice* within the individual/chorus scene; otherwise it may just head for an external catharsis - i.e. if a group repeats a phrase long and loud enough, a catharsis usually occurs, but is there any change?)

Intervention: People in the sculpt, all the Janes, say your phrases quietly and the chorus replies loud and firm; when I say switch, the Janes say the phrases loud and firm and the chorus quietly.

The group do this and a poignant dramatic interaction develops of the individual and the collective - the chorus is perfectly synchronised and the individuals shifting their physical position from weak to strong, (*Chris* and *John*) and from strong to weak (*Lenny*).

Intervention: Freeze; hold the sculpt for a moment - now relax and then move away from you position and change your body posture as you do so.

Lenny starts to cry, quietly and then more loudly - *Naomi* moves towards him - *Diana* says, 'he deserves it.'

Intervention: We are out of character now; take a few moments to leave the drama and be ourselves again.

Diana to *Joan*, 'thank you for your anger' - *Mary* 'I can share that' - *Naomi* 'it's so scary, all this violence' - *John* 'I rather enjoyed it' - *Chris* 'I wouldn't say that, but it's new' -

Intervention: I am aware that we've worked very intensively - do you want to process what we have done or to explore the other sculpt?

I'm exhausted - but Jimmy's fun, he'll cheer us up - it's hard work - do you think that he feels angry - he ran away to sea - let's give it a go -

Intervention: Let's create the sculpt and see what happens - I am aware that we are over half way through the group time.

After some brief checking out, the three men create the sculpt of Jimmy -

Lenny stands upright, feet apart, with his arms stretched out to the sides, slowly swaying from one foot to the other; *Chris* sits down cross legged and plays the flute, resting his back against *Lenny*, and *John* kneels on one knee, on the other side of *Lenny*, holding a telescope to one eye.

Lenny: I go with the sea, I'm free, free.

John: There's a storm up ahead.

Chris: Just listen to the music.

(*Teaching point*: The first impression can be that this is an idealised sculpt representing all the unattainable longings of the individuals and the group, far enough removed to stay as a fantasy and maintain the split, however:

1. fantasy and daydream are important;
2. aspects of them can be integrated;
3. unhelpful aspects can be transformed.

The transformative properties of the drama are important and are developed in dramatherapy to enable unhelpful roles to be transformed into more helpful roles.

What is the *sub-text* of this sculpt? My hunch is that it is in the storm - the *through line* is not clear to me, but may be clear to the members of the group if I ask them. The *super-objective* for these scenes is to acknowledge the struggle between dependence and independence. If I am correct, working with the storm will be appropriate.)

Intervention: Keep the sculpt, and I am asking the women to create the storm that Jimmy can see through the telescope.

The women go off into a corner and rapidly confer and experiment with some sweeping movements - they work together and turn towards the sculpt and move towards them making whooshing sounds and rocking movements - their movements get bigger and they give the impression of being enormous waves about to swamp the ship.

Intervention: Freeze for a moment - storm, what are you saying?

There's always a calm before a storm - watch out - we'll swallow you - we'll throw you into the deep water - we'll rock you gently - you'll all drown.

Intervention: Is it total destruction of Jimmy?

Silence - no - it's the ship - he's thrown into the water - he'll survive - but it's a big angry storm - he'll be washed up onto an island - *said the women*.
   He knows it's coming - it's his albatross - he never fought for that woman Jane - he's knocked off balance - but he doesn't lose the flute - he'll struggle in the water for a bit - but he'll be washed up - *said the men*.

(*Teaching point*: There is so much material here that is crucial to remember dramatic structure - my feeling is that it could end up as a free-for-all unless re-placed within the drama/theatre mode)

Intervention: OK - relax for a moment - we are introducing new elements and I want to be clear where to place them - you say there is an island - where is it?

Let's put one of the mats near the windows for the island - and some cushions - and a chair to be a tree - can we have some material for the waves and sea?

The long pieces of chiffon are brought out and a large piece of blue cheese cloth. Two of the women hold the chiffon pieces and make violent storm movements with them; the others hold the blue cloth between them and make an advancing wave. The men seem encouraged to expand their image and put some chairs round them to simulate a boat. They then start the drama with the men repeating their phrases and the women creating their chorus of storm and sea phrases. The props have enabled them to stay within the dramatic idiom and pace the movement and sound. The storm builds up to a climax and covers the boat with the blue cloth; the women remove the chairs and the men struggle in the water and start to swim for the island, eventually rolling onto the shore. The women spontaneously decrease the storm and become waves lapping round the shore, humming gently. The scene comes to a close of its own volition.

Intervention:	Everyone relax where you are, get into a comfortable position and close your eyes. Imagine that you are on a beach, near the sea, relaxing under a blue sky; the sea is gently lapping, you can just hear it. Picture the scene in your mind's eye, the sea is calm and there are boats far away on the horizon. Allow yourself to relax and enjoy being in the moment. *Pause.* Now you are slowly going to wake up - take your time - start to stretch - slowly open your eyes - and when you are ready, come into a sitting position.

The group follows my instructions, rubs their eyes, *Lenny* has slept and others have been near it.

Intervention:	We need to transform the room back to how it usually is - can we de-role and distance ourselves from the sea spaces and come back to the circle.

Everyone slowly gets up, and dismantles the ship, folds up materials and places props back in their cupboards, and then returns to the circle. No-one seems to want to talk.

(*Teaching point*: It is important to ground everyone now - i.e. make sure that they feel on firm ground and sufficiently distanced from the drama to walk away as individuals.)

Intervention:	Does anyone want to say anything? We have fifteen minutes before we finish.

Lots to think about - I was really frightened when the sea came but then I knew I could swim - I like being the storm - I didn't want to stop - it reminded me of lots of other things, lots of storms - I had forgotten the sea could be calm - I wonder what Jimmy did on the island - met up with Jane of course - Tarzan and Jane.

There is some giggling and cheetah noises, and jokes about take me to your tree house.

Intervention:	It is nearly time to stop, could we just check out how everyone is feeling right now?

Diana:	I don't feel sick - I feel a bit scared but I'm OK.
Mary:	I don't feel so angry as when I arrived, but I wanted to have a meeting with Jimmy.

Chris: But you did - as the sea.

                    Mary looks surprised but seems content.

John: I'm still confused, lots of feelings milling around, I need time
                    to let it settle.

Jean: It is so good to be really angry.

Lenny: Well Naomi, you were right about the sea of tears - I didn't
                    know I could cry so much.

Naomi: And I didn't know I could be so strong.

Intervention: Let's think for a moment about what we have done as a play
                    - two scenes from a very moving drama, which started with
                    the photograph. If these two scenes are the middle of the play,
                    how do we think it will end? All the Janes have confronted the
                    parents, and all the Jimmys have encountered the sea and
                    survived. What now?

Maybe Jane shouldn't marry either of the brothers - she should get away on her own
- what about her children? - don't go back to the photo - stay with our play - well,
after the island, Jimmy gets back home after waiting weeks for a boat - it's a long
journey and he decides to settle down - he continues to play his flute - but he stops
running away - he meets Jane when she has been on her journey - and they become
very good friends - they don't get married - but they understand each other.

Intervention: Maybe we can all think about possible endings before we
                    meet again next week. Can we all sit still for a moment and
                    make sure that we are back in our own skin again and leave
                    the drama safely in this room. Only take away with you what
                    you feel you can carry. If anyone is feeling in poetic mood -
                    what about sea poems?

Can we continue this drama again next week - do another episode of this story - we
haven't worked out the beginning - the photograph was the beginning - well I'd like
to do more -

Intervention: Fine - let's see where we are with the story next week - we
                    may want to stay with sea or another episode in the life of the
                    family - or desert islands - let's see.

The group closes, everyone looks very tired but at ease in their eyes.

Group notes

The drama

I am amazed at the aesthetic development of this group in its grasp of the dramatic material - spontaneously using props and allowing themselves to come to a natural end. The sea image was extremely powerful and stayed with me as an archetypal image that resonated (*Tempest, Odyssey* - nearly introduced the Syrens - interaction with Lenny?) They are able to enter characters and work with them very authentically. Should we think about a performance at a later date?

The group

Much more trust and thereby risk-taking has developed in this group. They feel free to challenge each other but also to sustain and support each other.

Therapist's reflections

This group has stretched me in all my faculties - at times I feel I'm holding a time-bomb - the sea image is an extremely powerful one which resonates with *The Tempest - Odyssey* - nearly introduced the Syrens. It is a re-affirmation of the importance of the internal artist which has seen me through the difficult journey. Also a reminder to keep myself replenished - although I had not thought of re-reading *The Turn of the Screw.*

As we can see, much of the material in these groups is 'family work' where people are able to explore difficult times in their lives and re-work their experience in dramatic form. What happens when dramatherapy is used with a family in situ? Families who come into therapy, as well as having individual issues to re-work, have family dramas that have become stuck. Often they will re-play the family dynamics within the therapy session and present an entrenched position. As family therapists point out, change in a single member does not necessarily bring about useful change in the family as a whole, unless all family members attend for therapy.

The dramatherapeutic methods described in this book are all useful ways of working with families, and the dramatic scenario enables sufficient dramatic distance from an often volatile situation. Themes from plays and myths, as well as scripts themselves, masks, sculpts, photographs, even costumes are all family media.

The Brown family attended for a single dramatherapy session as an adjunct to the marital counselling and child psychotherapy already in progress. Mr and Mrs Brown, Penny 7 years, and Jean 10 years, came for a two hour session, I had met them previously for an explanatory interview.[5] I invited them to play with the materials on the table (environmental object which include damp sand, stones, flowers, twigs, nuts, acorns, shells). The two girls readily climbed onto chairs and started examining everything, their parents paused for a few moments and then Mrs Brown drew up a chair, looking uncomfortable, and Mr Brown suggested that his younger daughter could sit on his knee. However I had said at the first meeting that every one was free to play how they wished, so I reminded them of that and suggested they all had their own chair. Mrs Brown picked up a twig and started scoring parallel lines in the sand; Mr Brown looked at everything, laughed nervously and then took some stones and placed them in a long line from one end of the table to the other, Penny scooped the sand into a pile, and decorated it with flowers, Jean concentrated on trying to balance some shells and stones on top of each other. They kept falling down, but she persisted. After the fourth attempt, her mother sighed in exasperation but did not say anything, and placed acorns in rows in between her parallel lines. Penny protested when her father placed the stones too near her hill and his wife gave him a look as if to say, 'and don't come near me'. Jean managed to balance her stones with the help of two vertical twigs, and looked very pleased. I suggested they made up a story about the places they had made.

Penny	Once upon a time there was a beautiful place with lots of flowers and everyone was very happy, (she looked at her mother), then one day the dragon came and frightened everyone.
Jean	So the princess hid away so that the dragon could not eat her, and she just did her sewing like Rapunzel. Go on, Mum, your turn.
Mrs Brown	.... Well the maid kept everything very neat and tidy, she was very busy because everyone made such a mess.
Mr Brown	So the man went for a walk along the path looking for a playmate, (he used two of his fingers to walk down the path).
Penny	Go away, go away, said the little girl. You mustn't come near the lovely flowers, you must go and kill the dragon so the children aren't frightened any more.
Jean	(*who picks flower petals into a pile and sprinkles them over everyone's picture as she talks*), so the man and the cleaning lady got married, and she turned into a queen so was very happy. That's all.
	What about the dragon?

Penny   The man got his sword and killed the dragon so everyone
                 could be happy again.

There is, in this play and story, a wealth of sub-text which did not need to be
interpreted. The children were able to express both their need for the parents to care
for each other, and also to protect the children. Mr Brown expressed his loneliness
and Mrs Brown her low self image. The first time I saw any animation on her face
was when Jean said the maid turned into a queen. My task in this situation was not
to offer explanations but to try to provide a structure to free communication between
the family members and enable them to establish appropriate boundaries. It was Mrs
Brown at the end of the session who asked if they could come and play again, at
which her husband was very surprised. We decided that if their other therapists
agreed, they could attend in a month's time.

This chapter illustrates 'ways in' to the drama and various methods to develop
material. It shows how limits and boundaries are established and the 'thinking
through' that is so important for the therapist. It is a golden rule - do not try to force
the unconscious either with yourself or with the people with whom you work. The
unconscious is very efficient in bringing to the surface what is needed, and the drama
provides the facilitating structure.

> '1ST GIRL: Don't be so traumatic.
> 2ND GIRL: What do you mean, traumatic?
> 1ST GIRL: You know, always exaggerating everything.
> 2ND GIRL: You mean dramatic, it's all a drama - and anyway
>   I'm not.'
>
> *overheard in a train*

Chapter Five

Dramatherapy with Individuals

'I can take any empty space and call it a bare stage. A man walks across this empty space whilst someone else is watching him, and this is all that is needed for an act of theatre to be engaged.'

Peter Brook: The Empty Space, p 11

It is usually assumed that dramatherapy is a group activity for small closed groups, slow open groups, large groups and medium groups; groups in all the models that we have discussed in the first four chapters. Some practitioners are surprised when they realise that one-to-one dramatherapy is a possible choice, depending on the needs of the client.[1]

Although we can compare this with the choices for clients referred for psychotherapy, I am aware that some therapists do not believe in choice but have a preferred ideological mode of psychotherapeutic/psychoanalytic practice, but there are some particular considerations that have to be made in relation to group/individual dramatherapy. First of all, many dramatherapists have an in-built response that one-to-one work must necessarily be verbal, or that drama is not possible unless there are several people present. There is a wide spectrum of dramatherapeutic methods appropriate for one-to-one sessions, including embodiment, projection and role techniques. However, clients usually need longer to habituate to this active method of work. An invitation to 'show me how your family looks' (instead of telling me about it), is a useful way in to the use of sculpting. Secondly, dramatherapists are divided on the usefulness or otherwise of the therapists entering different roles within the clients' drama. Just as people are referred for individual psychotherapy, as an alternative to a group or as a preliminary before entering a group, we can consider dramatherapy in exactly the same way. The difference will be that the communication will not only be through words but movement, images, symbols, expressed through the drama both verbally and non-verbally.

Most of the drama may take place from the client's chair - certainly in the early sessions. As in any other therapy (as I explained in Chapter Two), clients need to have the norms of the therapy explained and to have some habituation to the methods used.

Dramatherapy may be seen as appropriate for someone who has difficulty articulating their problems or for someone who uses words as a defence and for whom there appears 'no way through.' So we may decide not to use words or to use them minimally or to use the words of someone else, for example from a play or story.

Styles of working with individuals varies with the practitioner. For example, we may want to consider the therapist working 'in role' which we can weigh up in relation to individual philosophies of practice. Do we also work 'in role' with our dramatherapy groups?

When we begin our session with an individual and the client arrives, we are already in role as therapist and they are in role as a client coming to a dramatherapy session. We have to be very careful that the essential supportive 'being there' for the client does not become endangered if we take on other sorts of role as well. In early sessions I do not either go into role or expect clients to go into role. I spend several sessions exploring the here and now reasons that the client has for attending therapy. Gradually, I introduce an increasing number of dramatic methods as the client becomes slowly habituated to what is usually a new way of exploring his or her life.

The client usually attends regular therapy sessions in order to explore their world in the context of their own history. This exploration includes disabling factors which may impede her or him living their world to its fullest potential.

Very often I will start the work by asking the client how they see their world, right now; this may be expressed through a picture (finger or brush painting), through modelling (in plasticine or clay), through sand-pictures, or through sculpting using a variety of small objects and animals. I described in Chapter Four a range of dramatherapy methods that can be adapted to group or individual work.

When someone creates a representation of how they see their life, it is how they see it right now, and may be influenced - especially in an early session - by anxiety, wanting to please the therapist, wanting to do it 'right'. However the client may already have created some sculpts in the diagnostic sessions and so be used to variations of the method. You will find that the client very often wants you to explain the picture and tell them what it means. It needs to be made clear in the beginning, in the contract, that the aim of the sessions is to explore something together rather than explain things.

When a client creates a sculpt or other life picture, they have entered into a dramatic structure, created a scene in the drama of their life like a miniature theatre.

We must be aware that it can be a scene at any point of the client's play, not necessarily the opening scene.

So, for example, when a client was referred for anxiety about food and compulsive food rituals, this affected her whole life to the extent that she could not go to any spaces where she thought people might have been sick (underground stations, public houses etc.). She was very verbal and spent an entire session telling me about her food problem, how guilty she felt about it, how worthless she felt, how lacking in self-discipline she was when she ate three biscuits with her bed-time drink the night before.

I had a range of image making materials in the room and asked the client what she would like to work with. She looked distressed at the thought of finger-paint and said that it would get up her nails, and so would the plasticine, and the sand and water would be messy. She looked at the range of small different objects (people animals, abstract etc.), and I suggested that she work with the animals, wanting to encourage her away from people play and knowing that she could reject the suggestion if it threatened her. She examined all the small wild animals in the box and thoughtfully chose three. She ignored any other materials such as the gates, trees, shells and stones. She placed the three small animals on the desk.

In creating the sculpt, she had chosen a hippopotamus to represent herself, an owl to represent her husband, and a fox-cub for her son of five years. They were placed in an empty space, with the owl and fox close together and the hippopotamus more distant; the owl and the fox had their backs towards the hippopotamus. I asked if these creatures had anything else in their landscape and she took the stones and created a circle of jagged rocks round the animals. It was extremely difficult for her to make the shift to talking about the animals instead of always referring back to herself; for example, she said, 'Well, I chose the hippopotamus for me because I feel so swollen and big, and Peter, he is the owl because he is so wise, much wiser than I am...'

This is a way of exploring but more closely resembles reportage as discussed in Chapter Two - that is, create a picture and then say what it is. It needs very careful shifts of question to try and move into the dramatic mode. On this occasion I asked her to describe the circle of rocks.

Therapist:	Tell me about the rocks.
Client:	They are very tall and black and keep out the sun-light; they stop me -
Therapist:	They stop the hippopotamus...
Client:	Yes of course. They stop the hippopotamus seeing the sun because her, I mean the owl, doesn't like the sun anyway and

Animal sculpt

the fox and the owl are very happy in the valley surrounded by rocks.

Therapist:	How does the hippopotamus feel?
Client:	Well, it is very frightening; there is no water and no sun; the hippo feels cold and dry, and so, so heavy.[2]
Therapist:	Do the animals ever make any journey?
Client:	Well, of course the owl can fly, so it's easy for him, he flies right over those mountain tops into the land beyond, and the hippo has to stay right behind.

(*Teaching point*: Already there is a wealth of material to be worked with here but it is too soon; some more safety needs to be established first).

Therapist:	So where do all these animals shelter?
Client *(pausing)*:	...Well, there isn't anywhere really - not that you'd call safe; but they must have somewhere - right - they have a cave in the rockside - see that place there, well that goes into the mountain but the animals just stay inside.
Therapist:	Does the hippopotamus feel safe in there?
Client *(pause)*:	Well, not really - it's very dark in there, and the darkness stretches way back inside the mountain; there are lots of shadows.
Therapist:	Can the hippopotamus add something to make it feel a bit safer?
Client:	*(Silent, and then casting around the room, and then looking back at the picture again, then hesitantly she takes tree and places it at the base of the rock)* There, that's better; the tree makes some shade and the hippo can lie in the protection of the branches.
	(She then places the hippopotamus under the tree, the owl on top of one of the stones, and the fox across the circle at the foot of another stone).
Therapist:	So the hippopotamus is feeling better now?
Client:	Yes, and the owl has come back from across the mountain and the fox has gone off for a walk. The hippo is taking a nap and the owl is just watching.
Therapist:	*(After a pause while the client sits looking at the picture, her body looking a little more relaxed than it did earlier)* It is

time for the hippopotamus to wake up and for all the animals
to go away until next time.

Client: *(Demolishing the picture very quickly and putting things back
                 into the basket)* Well, that's that. *(She stands up and leaves
                 the room very quickly, saying as she opens the door)* The
                 hippo does need that tree; see you next week.

Thinking through: The images are very rich: of the black jagged stones; the cave
which is dark with shadows; no sunlight; trapped; the owl that can fly away; the land
beyond; no water; my client is very thin and she chooses a hippopotamus to represent
herself, stuck with no water and no sun; food has not been mentioned at all in this
session.

Rationale: I said earlier that safety needed to be established; the landscape that this
client created was fearful and bleak with no positive images; by allowing her to
create even minimal safety it both gave her some autonomy and created minimal
safety. Especially remembering that this person is attending a dramatherapy session
once a week with no support system in between, I was struck by the tree creating
shadow and there being no sun anyway, and the theme of shadows. My own
associations brought to mind *A Midsummer Night's Dream*, Lorca and *Pirandello*:

> 'MARTIRIO: I have a heart full of a force so evil that, without
>   my wanting to be, I'm drowned by it.'
>
>   *Lorca: House of Bernarda Alba, III*

> 'To you your father should be as a god;
> One that composed your beauties - yea, and one
> To whom you are but as a form in wax
> By him imprinted, and within his power
> To leave the figure or disfigure it.'
>
>   *Shakespeare: A Midsummer Night's Dream. I.i*

> 'STEPDAUGHTER *(coming down the stage as if in a dream)*:
>   It's true, I would go, would go and tempt him, time after
>   time, in his gloomy study just as it was growing dark,
>   when he was sitting quietly in an armchair not even
>   bothering to switch light on but leaving the shadows to
>   fill the room: the shadows were swarming with us, we had

come to tempt him. *(As if she could see herself there in the study and is annoyed by the presence of the ACTORS)* Go away will you! Leave us alone! Mother there, with that son of hers - me with the little girl - that poor little kid always on his own - and then me with him *(pointing to the FATHER)* and then at last, just me, on my own, all on my own, in the shadows. *(She turns quickly as if she wants to cling on to the vision she has of herself, in the shadows)* Ah, what scenes, what scenes we suggested to him! What a life I could have had! I tempted him more than the others!

Pirandello: *Six Characters In Search Of An Author, III.i*

Thinking through for the next session
I had some concerns that the client had left so abruptly but felt that she had left with the positive image of the tree; I was struck by her choice of the tree to give the hippopotamus shade when there was no sun; I felt that she presented a picture of the darknesses - the cave and the circle of rocks, she is already in the darkness (I remembered a Joan Sutherland interview when she talked about giving up her singing so that she could 'embrace her darknesses'). Should we explore the tree? Or a source of light? Could the hippopotamus travel beyond the mountain? How much was an expression of sexual imagery OR is the sexual imagery a way of talking about many other things? The Pirandello scenario keeps coming back into consciousness.

Whereas pyschotherapists will often recall particular theorists, - Winnicott said..., or case histories; dramatherapists recall themes from dramatic works of art - plays, performances, myths images, metaphors, symbols.

Dramatherapists need to keep the images free-floating rather than searching for *the* explanation - the scenario and the images that are relevant usually impinge and will not go away (see Chapter Four, *The Turn of the Screw*).

For example, with the associations with Pirandello's *Six Characters*, it would be easy for me to make a chain of associations and consider that the client was like the step-daughter and perhaps there was an association with the father...

The step-daughter is the most dramatic character in the play - but there is also the one who *isn't seen* - the older son - the reluctant one - the one who stays with his father - the two small children, silent - one of whom dies at the end? The client had talked about lack of freedom, no sun, the hippo being big and swollen - 'you can't miss a hippo' - yet this woman is so very thin - dresses in a way not to be noticed - shame is a word that comes to mind, (and shame is one of the sub-texts in *Six Characters*).

She arrives for her session early and comes into the room looking anxious and wary. 'Right, what do you want to know?' This was a shift back to an earlier mode when she said to me 'You ask me questions and I'll answer them.' I said 'Shall we explore some more pictures or do you want to talk about other things? - she wavered, looked round the room, then at me and said, 'I don't think this therapy is getting very far; it's getting off the subject; we haven't talked about food and being sick and I really am so disgusted with myself I have no discipline.' Her voice went higher and higher and tears welled up. I waited and she began to howl.

The crying stopped and she looked across at me and said, 'You make me bloody sick - I am so angry - I have had a terrible week - I've screamed at Michael, and Peter - I broke some glasses and pretended it was an accident - I've got to get better - I can't be disciplined enough, however hard I try -'

Therapist:	Who sets a good example of discipline for you that you model yourself on?
Client:	Michael of course - he is so honest - and my father. I'll never be as disciplined as they are.
Therapist:	And who do you see as undisciplined?
Client:	My mother - she is so fat and ugly and always crying.
Therapist:	If we looked at the animals again, which animal would you choose to represent your parents?
Client:	*(She hesitated a few moments and then looked through and talked to herself as she handled different creatures - you won't do, you are too small, and you have such teeth, and you are too nice...she then chose a cow lying down and a wolf with a red tongue.)* This cow is my mother because it's fat and passive and the wolf is strong - always alert and ready - and defends what is right - I don't know how they manage to live together.
Therapist:	Shall we create a story about how the cow and wolf live together - the fat and passive cow and the alert, strong, wolf, defender of rights?
Client:	OK, yes - *(she suddenly smiled at this idea)* where shall we start?
Therapist:	How about if you tell the story and I write it down and help if it gets stuck?
Client:	Right - how shall I start?

Second session animals

Therapist:	Well, we could start by saying where and when this story takes place.
Client:	Once upon a time - it was a dark and stormy night - and the wolf who lived in the forest was very restless (*she giggles*) the old fat cow who looks after him is was is snoring very loud...and, and...dribbling down her chin - and the wolf is fed up with all this and decides to go out of the cave into the shadowy forest.

(She pauses and looks at me)

Therapist:	Describe the forest a bit more?
Client:	Well - it is very dark, and the trees are tall and old the moon is giving a little light - all the little forest animals are asleep and hiding - especially the rabbit - the wolf smells the rabbit and starts to sniff round the tree, its red tongue hanging out and stinking breath - the rabbit is petrified and holds its breath in the dark - at last the wolf goes away but the rabbit is frightened that it might come back.
Therapist:	What is the cow doing now?
Client:	The cow - it doesn't know anything - it just sleeps and snores - and dribbles - and then wakes up and eats a lot. It's a disgusting cow. No wonder the wolf tried to escape - anyway, the wolf came back in the morning and carried on as normal - working hard and looking after the family. That's the story.

I read her back her story and she listened to it very intently and asked if she could have a copy of it, to which I agreed. It was time for the session to finish. She put away the animals more slowly and said 'see you next week - maybe we'll tell the second chapter'.

It was important for the client to be in touch with her fear through the image of the rabbit and the feelings of helplessness in relation to this powerful figure that she idolised. In the story the parental figures are completely split between good/disciplined father and weak/disgusting mother - she sees herself as fat and disgusting (hippopotamus) in the picture of her own family, yet in her parents' family she identifies herself with the petrified rabbit.

Notice how the client shifts from the past to the present tense in the story and stays very much within the animal metaphor, unlike the previous session. However, it is the image of the forest that enables her to get into the fear and acknowledge its reality. Notice, too, how she graphically describes the dribbling and the breath and used the same expressions when she described her own vomiting. This session was a major shift for this client who had many more chapters to tell in this story - she spoke, modelled and drew characters and settings from this story. Many weeks later, she came to her session and said, 'I'm ready to tell you about the abuse now - the rabbit has a bit of courage'.

Working with adolescents

It is often assumed that dramatherapy is a means of working through personal issues that either worry the adolescent, concern the therapist or give rise to anxiety in the family and/or society. The perceptions of the adolescent by her or himself, and others, may all vary. For example, there is the young person whose family presents them as a problem, and the young person does not experience it; or society may experience both the young person and the family as a problem and neither experience it.

Where does one start in this daunting multiple perception of the present adolescent? Whatever referral notes I may receive, I often find it useful in a diagnostic session to allow the adolescent to work with several perceptions from their own view. A typical session is as follows.

Eddie was fourteen and had been referred for dramatherapy as being 'impossible at home'. The family said that life consisted just of arguments and the provocation of younger sibling. Life had been a little quieter since he had started boarding school, but the problems were heightened in the holidays so things to do were organised as much as possible; school reported that he was a loner and did not make friends, academically he was above average, but was very intolerant of his peer group.

Eddie presented for his first session on time, easy of manner, looking younger than his chronological age:

Eddie:	Everyone says it's a good idea for me to see you because of problems at home.
Therapist:	Problems at home?
Eddie:	Well...yes...I and my mother are always rowing...about the stupidest things...and she says she can't cope.
Therapist:	That's what your mother says. What about you?
Eddie:	I don't see that there is a problem really. It's always been tricky with my mother, but she's so unreasonable, so touchy; she flies off the handle at the slightest thing.

It was quite evident to me that Eddie was very articulate, probably beyond his years, although looking less than his age. My hunch was that in pictorial expression he would be less mature since it would involve less control. The strategy was to test whether my hunch about pictorial expression was correct (ie projection) and if it was, to capitalise on his verbal expression and use it to explore the different perceptions of himself *and his family*.

Therapist:	Let's use felt pens and paper for you to make a picture of your family.
Eddie:	I'm hopeless at drawing apart from technical drawing.
Therapist:	The idea is not to produce a 'good' picture but for you to show me your family.
Eddie:	It really is difficult - I'm no good at drawing - but I'll have a try.

He proceeded to draw his family in a line - father, mother, himself and younger sister, talking as he went along. 'I'm not good at drawing faces' 'that's what she wears...' The drawing was reminiscent of the drawing of a ten-year-old.

Eddie:	Here - it's really not much good is it?
Therapist:	Tell me about the different members of your family.

Eddie pointed to each of the pictures and gave a thumb-nail sketch. This is still the descriptive stage, ie the programme notes describing the characters, necessary before moving into *role*.

Therapist:	You said at the beginning that everyone said it's a good idea for you to see me because of the problems. Let's imagine that you are each member of the family and saying why Eddie needs to come here...Who shall we start with?
Eddie:	Well, it's no good starting with my father because he agrees with my mother.
Therapist:	So what would he say?
Eddie:	*(Spontaneously leaning back and crossing his arms and legs)* Well dear, if you think it's best, I leave it to you.

At a later session, we would explore what father had *not* been saying but perhaps feeling.

Therapist:	Who is going to talk now?
Eddie:	Well my sister is just silly. She just says stupid things in front of her friends.
Therapist:	Such as?

Eddie:	*(Raising his voice and pouting)* That's my stupid brother. He won't let us go into his room because of his computer. *(In his own voice)* And then they all go off giggling. My mother is more difficult - she's so dramatic - always raising her voice saying thing like 'You're quite impossible - I give up'.
Therapist:	What voice does she use when she says that? Try saying it again.
Eddie:	*(Spontaneously hands on his hips)* I'm not telling you again. I won't have you speaking to me like that. Why haven't you got any friends to play with like your sister?
Therapist:	And now what are you saying in this scene?
Eddie:	*(Lowering voice and setting shoulders hunched)* I only want to *talk* to you...you never have any time for me.
Therapist:	So Eddie in this scene is feeling very lonely?
Eddie:	Mmmm...yes. *(Suddenly in his own voice)* But not all the time though.
Therapist:	So let's look at another scene where you don't feel lonely.

Eddie proceeded to describe a scene before he went to boarding school when there was a family holiday at his grandmother's, and his grandmother and he had got on very well together. We *voiced* the characters again.

In the above scene we can see the progression from:

1. Generalised description (very common with adolescents - nobody understands me; everybody hates me).

2. Pictorial expression (focus for talking about).

3. Talking 'about' the situation (programme notes for scene).

4. Becoming the situation (engagement in role).

Note how once *in role* I did not refer to Eddie as *you* but as Eddie. This is the point of transition into the *dramatic convention* which allows sufficient distancing and thus greater freedom of expression (Scheff, 1979, Landy 1986).

This is a brief example which both illustrates the possibilities of dramatherapy in one-to-one situations, and also the diagnostic value of dramatherapy when assessing a person for therapy.[3]

These two case histories illustrate the potential of dramatherapy in the one-to-one setting in relation to medium and long-term therapy as well as being important diagnostically. It is important that the dramatherapist holds the situation as well allowing a free-ranging energy across many images and symbols as the client struggles to stay in the creative moment - in the now. The noticeable shift in the first client was her eventual transition from reportage, question and answer to image making and story telling. She was eventually able to trust a structure over which she herself did not have total control. Of course it is possible to associate images concerning the abuse in the early sessions but she had to be ready to tell her story in her own time.

There are more examples of individual work in the following chapter on special application, and more elaboration on the needs of the dramatherapist in Chapter Seven.

When a client attends for individual dramatherapy work they must be able to bring not only all of themselves but the rest of the people that inhabit their world. In Jennings and Minde (1990) we describe how the arts therapist enables the client to retain what is appropriately theirs and discard what does not belong to them. The dramatherapy scenario in its fullest sense enables the client to acknowledge and own their own darknesses and also to shed what belongs elsewhere.

'This thing of darkness I acknowledge mine.'

Shakespeare: The Tempest. V.i

Chapter Six

Masking and Unmasking: the interface of dramatherapy

> 'Thou knowest the mask of night is on my face,
> Else would a maiden blush bepaint my cheek...'
>
> *Shakespeare: Romeo and Juliet II.ii*

No account of dramatherapy practice is balanced without an understanding of the use of masks. Mask work can be very powerful both in the theatre and therapeutically. This has led some practitioners to avoid mask-work, fearing its potential dangers. The 'danger' that such people speak of, is that of people losing the boundaries between fantasy and reality; of a mask stirring or imposing uncontrollable emotions; or a person being unable to 'de-role' or distance from a mask, once the drama has ended and the mask been removed.

Some people have reported that they have worked with people who have been unable to take off the mask at the end of a session. I address all these points in this chapter and give clear guidelines, structures and mask forms that are suitable for therapeutic application. Perhaps the most fundamental of these guidelines is my earlier maxim, that no therapist should attempt mask work until they have both made masks and worked with them for themselves.

Having stated this, I also think that there are many fantasies associated with mask work, which may partly stem from people having had unfortunate experiences themselves. These accounts bear many similarities to reports of some peoples' discomfort when they have been involved in role-play. It usually turns out that insufficient preparation was done by the group leader to habituate participants to this way of working, (either masks or role-play); that people were pushed too fast or too far or that endings were sudden and harsh.

Such an example was illustrated when I was conducting a two day workshop for post-graduate psychologists in a teaching hospital and had worked on the first day with embodiment and projection. The students had made good use of developing their non-verbal expression through movement, gesture and sculpting - such as being able to physicalise the essence of a scene rather then verbalise it. They had created mini-sculpts of their own lives and client situations and in my mind were ready to progress to exploring these situations through role-play.

When I suggested this as the task for the second day, the group as a whole blanched and said that they did not want to do role-play. We discussed this in a course meeting and they then explained that two weeks previously a senior member of staff had been using role-play to explore problem families. The students had been asked to devise families, allocate roles, and then play the scenes. Without warning, the tutor had looked at his watch, and said, 'Gosh, we *are* running late; right, everyone, stop and have a lunch break'. The students were abandoned both *in role* and *in scene*, in situations that had been highly emotive and had brought them in touch with a lot of their own personal feelings. They still felt very vulnerable from the experience.

I describe this incident in order to illustrate the type of anxiety some people have as a result of being in the hands of professional people who ought to know better. It is only comparatively recently that more and more psychologists and family therapists are realising that they need to know far more about drama and theatre and the dramatic process if they want to use drama methods in their work. There are still, however, psychologists who feel they have a prerogative on role-playing expertise, or who have not grasped that role-playing is a part of drama which needs drama/theatre expertise. Drama does not just belong to the dramatherapists, as I said earlier, and is therefore available to a range of disciplines. Perhaps the traditional British temperament gets in the way of this understanding of an art form as a part of an academic/clinical body of knowledge (see Chapter One).[1] The dangers for the uninitiated lie in their assumption that dramatic methods can be used purely from book-learning and not from personal experience and training; or when clinicians suggest that role-play has nothing to do with drama.

Incidentally, with the above group I worked initially on their ability to distance from the family situations and then made use of the public/private mask method (described later in this chapter). We explored the public face of being a post-graduate 'professional' and the expectations that it carried with it contrasted with the private mask through which they were able to express their fears, anxieties and concerns about being a good-enough psychologist; of 'measuring-up' as one student said. It was interesting that wearing their private masks they used psychological language to express their self-doubt; for example, 'will I ever pass the test?'; 'I am scared I won't measure up'; 'this is a real testing time'. This example begins to demonstrate the usefulness of focussed mask-work.

We can see therefore, that antipathy towards the use of masks can stem from peoples' own unfortunate experiences; from legendary stories, such as 'someone at the hospital where I worked, told me about an incident when masks were used and the patients became very violent and had to be medicated'; and sometimes from peoples' unease that masks are too 'primitive', perhaps having connections with spirit possession and evil demons. Some authorities in mainstream theologies feel very uneasy about masks and in the past have banned them as pagan practice. In my early anthropological research when I researched the 'kuda kepang', the hobby horse dance done by Javanese migrants in Malaysia (Jennings, 1973), Muslim Malays were not happy about pre-Muslim rituals and the masks were described as being 'for fun', 'just a play'. In the morality plays, it is Satan, the force of evil, and not Christ who wears a mask.

Keith Johnstone (1981) suggests that anti-mask feeling is really anti-trance feeling, and that Western culture is very hostile to trance. He says:

> '...this culture is hostile to trance states. We distrust sponta-
> neity, and try to replace it by reason: the Mask was driven
> out of the theatre in the same way that improvisation was
> driven out of music. Shakers have stopped shaking. Quakers
> don't quake any more. Hypnotised people used to stagger
> about, and tremble. Victorian mediums used to rampage
> about the room. Education itself might be seen as primarily
> an anti-trance activity.'
>
> *Johnstone: Impro: Improvisation and the Theatre, p 149*

I do not wish to discuss in detail here the nature of trance states. However, in many therapeutic states and in focussed every-day states, different degrees of trance-like experience occur without comment. We can be so involved in a story we are reading that we do not notice that it has turned dark outside and we are straining to read; we suddenly come to and re-engage with the wider world and our own senses. This happens when our attention is narrowed down and focussed, (what Johnstone calls 'absorption') so that we become unaware of other external stimuli such as people coming into the room, changes in bodily temperature, a thunder storm and so on. We have all had experience of the focussed and selective listening of the mother of a new-born baby - she can sleep through tornadoes but will awake at the slightest murmur from the child.

When we are engaged in drama, we are stepping into dramatic reality as we have already described. We are thus in a focussed state that has all the qualities of conscious trance. It varies with the degree of involvement in the activity or the character being played. Masks are one way of assisting this greater focus on the theme, image or character. A mask also enables the transformation from a person's everyday self into the character.

It is the paradox of the mask that it both conceals and reveals: it conceals individual identity and reveals either hidden aspects of the individual or a collective representation of a class, profession or deity.

Thus a surgeon wearing a mask in an operating theatre is no longer Mr Jones but the doctor or the surgeon, that is, a representative of the profession of surgeons (the parallels between operating theatres and theatrical theatres make a fascinating study, see Jennings 1991). An actor in Greek tragedy becomes the chorus or Zeus, rather than an individual human character. The mask of the hangman or terrorist conceals the individual's identity for self-protection, yet the mask itself is recognised as representing membership of a sub-group.

Therefore, when we use masks therapeutically we have to be clear about the focus of the mask work. We may choose to use the masks so that a person may explore different aspects of themselves. We may decide to work through dramatic distance with a story, myth or play, where masks represent different elements, the forces of nature, constellations, mythic characters and so on. People get in touch with various aspects of themselves in both modes. What we need to remember is that the nearer we work to a person's own life, i.e. the more proximity, the more limitations we impose on the exploration of their life story. The greater the dramatic distance we create, the greater the range of therapeutic choices possible. There are examples of both kinds of work in this chapter.

Before giving actually examples of mask work in practice, I want to discuss a range of mask forms and the rationale for their use. There is a great range of masks, both pre-formed and those that people create, and we need to be clear about the appropriateness of their use.

Teaching point: Mask work must be introduced gradually into dramatherapeutic groupwork and patients need to become habituated to method. There are some very firm guidelines concerning mask application.

1. Apart from the simple diagnostic mask work, never use masks early in a group's development.

2. Start with a mask that does not cover the face (that can be hand-held, or on a pole like a puppet).

3. Make use of hats with low brims or veils.

4. Work with masks that only cover the eyes.

5. Never leave people in masks for more than a few minutes.

6. Always allow time for disengaging and distancing from a mask, and becoming oneself again.

The masks on the following page (figure 1) illustrate a mask progression from the most simple to the more complex. All can be created by group members.

Mask progression:

  — Pole-puppet - mask on a stick with a cloth: can be held in front of the face or to the side.
  — Fan-masks - raffia or paper fans can be painted to use as hand-held masks (hairdressers' lacquer masks can be used in the same way).
  — Head band with wool, raffia, etc. knotted in lengths to cover the face.
  — mask to cover eyes only.
  — 1/3 mask with human/animal nose or beak.
  — mask covering the cheeks but not nose.
  — 2/3 mask covering front of face; (tied or held).
  — Whole face mask that covers under the chin.
  — Whole head mask that covers most of the head

Teaching point: Be exceptionally careful when progressing to the last two kinds of mask - whole face and whole head. At this point people are completely enclosed in a mask like a second skin; identification is strongest at this point.

The 2/3 mask can be made from card; I use a basic mask template made from stout card with just the eye-holes cut out. People can then draw round it onto card and create their own mask shapes. The card masks can be developed with crayon, paint, stuck-on materials and so on.

Private and public masks

Each person in the group creates two card masks. Ask them to close their eyes and to think about the mask that the world sees, their public mask; then ask them to think about a more private mask, that perhaps fewer people see.

Teaching point: You are ensuring here that the private mask is not going too deep, too quickly. That is, you have said that it is a mask that is also seen; also they are reflecting on both these masks at the same time.

Ask people to open their eyes and to create first the public and then the private masks (for variations see also Jennings 1986 pp 166-172). People can share their public then their private mask in the group, or in pairs. They can set up a scene which is played through the masks. They can look at the connections between the two masks and share what they would like to change. Partners can introduce each other through

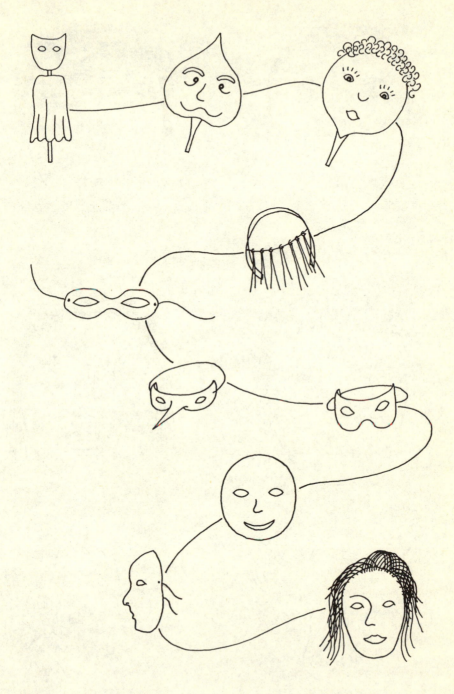

Figure 1: Mask progression

Figure 2

Figure 3

Figure 4

the masks. It is important that people are able to move between the two masks and be aware of changes in feeling in the two states. Very often there is a lot of tension in the public mask; it is a face that many people strain to maintain. Conversely there is often a release in the private mask and people may feel like crying (see figure 2).

People find that through experimenting with different masks and the roles that go with them, they can discover new ways of being. The private masks can express unacknowledged needs and feelings, such as loneliness, vulnerability, anger. In figure 3 we can see a public and a private mask created by a woman who has serious infertility problems. She talked about the public face she kept up, with which she was able to disguise the problem to everyone apart from her husband; she wore a lot of make up, kept her hair very neat, and indeed seemed to literally wear a mask when she went to work. She talked about the control of this mask, self-control. Her private mask shows her sadness and desperation, and she described how the open mouth showed her cry for help:

> 'No-one can help me - not even the doctors. I feel quite desperate - I must have a baby - I'll do *anything* to have a baby - I'm a mess - I hate being like this.'

Her husband then commented that he couldn't stand her being like this, he liked her neat and tidy self, it was what had attracted him to her in the first place. She started to cry again, and said:

> 'I can't show him how I really feel - he hates it - so I have to cry alone.'

Another member of the group asked the couple what they would do if they had a baby which cried and made a mess. The husband said:

> 'I'm not sure I really want a baby; it will change too many things.'

The wife said:

> 'My baby will be perfect - it does not have to make a mess.'

This couple needed to work long term on the various issues about wanting/not wanting a baby; confused expectations of each other and a baby; control and mess; the dream baby.

They stayed in a group for people with fertility problems but agreed that they would postpone treatment until some of their conflicts had been resolved. They subsequently realised that the major problems in the relationship had surfaced once the subject of babies became important.

Some months later, we re-explored masks again, and I asked the couples in the group to draw masks of their partners when they first met. The husband mentioned above did not draw a mask as it is shown in figure 3, but a softer, gentle mask with no make-up.

Dramatic distance

The above masks directly explore issues for clients and patients within their immediate realm of experience. It is possible to distance over time - eg. childhood or old age; or the archaic or futuristic; or distance through role. For example, people may create masks to represent themselves as if they were an animal (see figure 4). An even greater distance is created if the role is within the context of a myth or a story or a play.

I am of the belief that some feelings can only be expressed through masks - feelings that are too anti-social, dangerous or depressing to be shown in other ways. Masks can contain the feelings that could not otherwise be expressed.

Figure 5 shows a mask created by a person in a dramatherapy group. She says it represents how depressed she is. The group have been asked to create a mask to represent a feeling. The other group members have created masks of sadness, tears, anger, strength, confidence, and so on, but in relation to themes from the elements. We are working on seasons and constellations. This person has created a mask of her own feelings.

Teaching point: People may move between the individual, group and dramatic themes, and the dramatherapist needs to know the most appropriate mode for exploration.

With the above situation, I have to make a decision whether to stay with the individual feelings or whether to go back to the drama that the group evolves. To go into an individual's depression, especially through mask, can exacerbate the problem. So I asked her if the depression changed according to the seasons of the year or the time of day. She thought for a moment and said that winter and autumn were the worst times, and the middle of the night, when she could not sleep. The other members of the group had created sea, earth, and sun masks, so I asked her if her mask could also be a mask of night. She agreed that it could and became re-engaged with the group. The group evolved a creation myth of their own:

> 'Once upon a time a lonely pig went for a walk in the
> countryside. He sat down and felt very down and depressed
> and did not notice the sun was shining. He heard a whispering
> in the leaves which said to him, 'Go for a walk in the woods';
> he walked towards the woods and soon was in the shade of

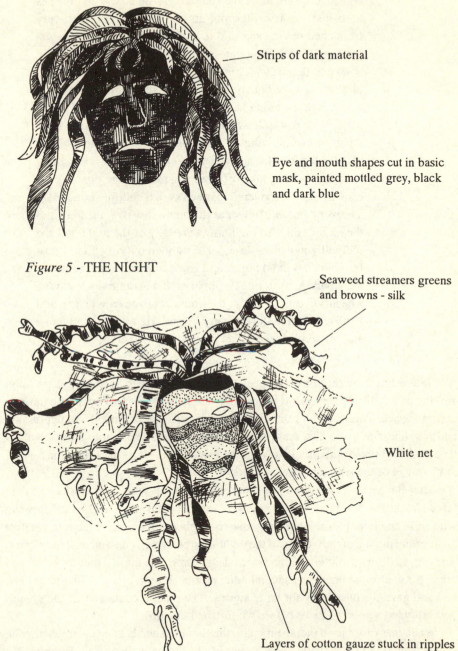

Strips of dark material

Eye and mouth shapes cut in basic
mask, painted mottled grey, black
and dark blue

Figure 5 - THE NIGHT

Seaweed streamers greens
and browns - silk

White net

Layers of cotton gauze stuck in ripples
painted shades of blue, grey and white

Figure 6 - THE SEA

the trees. He lay down and went to sleep. While he was asleep he had a dream about the sea; he was on a boat and the sea took him on a voyage out into the ocean. He was very frightened but the sea said to him 'Don't be afraid, the sea looks after you, soon you will be back on land again'. The wind and the sea took him back to the land, the earth helped him through the countryside and the sun warmed him after his voyage. Just then he woke up from his dream and it was night in the forest. It was very dark and all he could see were a pair of eyes shining through the dark. It was the owl, the spirit of the forest. The owl said 'Don't be afraid, everything is changing now, take off your pig mask'. The pig took off his mask and discovered that he was a beautiful young man. The wood became lighter as the moon rose over the trees and the moon said, 'You will meet the lady of the night and she will tell you many stories'. He wandered through the forest for many days and nights and came to a tree in the centre of the wood. A mysterious woman sat in the doorway, weaving a beautiful carpet. She said, 'Come here and sit with me, and I will tell you the stories in my carpet'. He went to the woman and sat and listened to her stories and then went on his way to a new land.'

It is interesting how the story encapsulates so many themes, including depression and the possibility of change - it is the pig who changes after his symbolic journey across the sea. The woman of the night is a witness to the change from depression and loneliness and she also contributes to the change. The whole story involves transition and transformation involving the basic elements of the earth, sun, moon, sea, woman of the night and owl messenger.

After the group had created this story we enacted it with their masks and then talked about the new land. What is the new land that we all want? 'A land flowing with milk and honey', someone immediately replied. I then asked them to create a large group picture of the woman of the night's carpet which contained all her stories. They created a huge picture within which they painted the masks, the story they had created and also the images of several other stories. It both brought the group to an end and gave the possibility for more stories. The picture contained all the images and provided a point of focus before we finished the group.

When masks are used therapeutically, the therapist needs to be clear whether he or she is working close to the client's own life or dramatically distant from it.

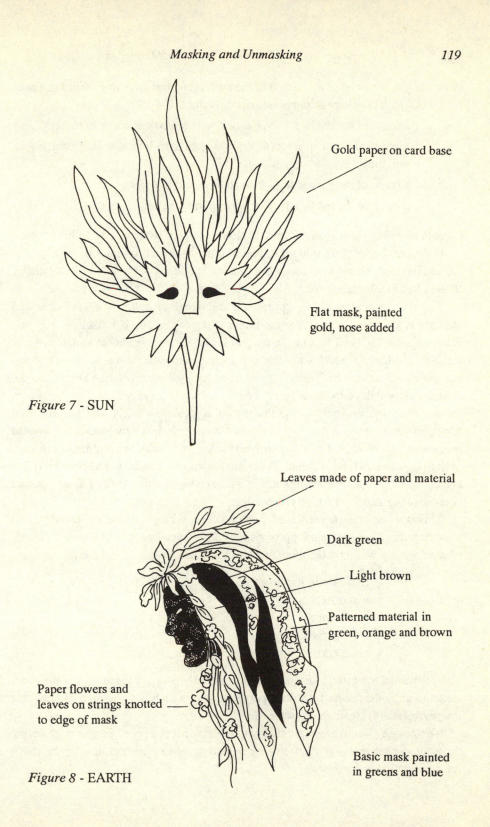

Gold paper on card base

Flat mask, painted
gold, nose added

Figure 7 - SUN

Leaves made of paper and material

Dark green

Light brown

Patterned material in
green, orange and brown

Paper flowers and
leaves on strings knotted
to edge of mask

Basic mask painted
in greens and blue

Figure 8 - EARTH

For example, if someone is referred to me suffering from an eating disorder, I may well work with the client's immediate mask images:

— a mask of themselves now, i.e. the person who has come to therapy;

— a mask of them in relation to food, (eg. starving, bingeing, stuffing or vomiting);

— a mask of their ideal self - how they would like to be;

— a mask of themselves past or present, that they like.

I would probably work with the card mask template, illustrated later in this chapter.

However, I may choose to work at dramatic distance through a scene or story. An ancient story that I sometimes use in such situations is the tale of *The Laidley Worm* (Northumberland).

The story concerns a king, queen, son and daughter; the son leaves home and the mother becomes ill and dies; the father is depressed and is looked after by his daughter; one day he is hunting in the forest and meets a beautiful woman who is actually a witch; he marries her and brings her home; the witch is jealous of the daughter and changes her into a disgusting worm; the worm starts to consume the countryside and devours the animals, and the villagers go to see the wise-person up the mountain; the wise person says that the villagers should take the milk from seven beautiful cows and feed it to the worm, but in order to be of real help, they should bring home her brother. The villagers feed milk to the worm, her brother sails home, goes to fight her and she tells him, in her human voice who she is. The brother kisses her and she becomes human again, the witch changes into a toad, and the brother becomes king and lives happily ever after.

This story contains several useful themes for working with eating disorder but I want to concentrate on the mask possibilities. This story can be used with individuals or with groups, whereby the main masks are created by the participant(s):

> four family members
> witch/step-mother
> giant worm
> wise-person
> villagers

The individual, or group, enacts episodes from the story. I usually give the story skeleton up to the point of the wise-person giving the advice, and then suggest that the participant(s) create their own ending.

The *Laidley Worm* story parallels many personal stories of people with eating disorder - father re-marrying, step-mother taking over - daughter developing problems in relation to food.

In work with individual patients, change can take place through the exploration of several of the masks: the mask of the step-mother, the wise person as well as the worm. The patient creates the masks through drawing, plasticine (the masks do not necessarily have to be worn and small mask models are often powerful enough for many people), or painting blank masks. It is interesting to discover that many people with eating disorders choose a blank mask to represent how they feel - 'I am just a nothing' - 'I am blank' - I am nobody'.[2]

This story enables people to create a dramatic distance between themselves and their life history; the masks enhance this process and provide an opportunity for the various internal and external roles to be explored and transformed into a more appropriate and integrated character. The worm mask enables them to create a distance between their *own eating disorder role* and the character they are playing. By receiving the unconditional succour of the prize cows, it is possible for the eating disorder/worm mask to be removed; however, lasting transformation can only take place if the patient has been able to *internalise the wise person, and let go of the parental relationship and establish a peer friendship of trust*.

The story itself allows the regression of the worm, and illustrates the unconditional love that is possible for the 'disgusting monster', (a phrase used by anorectic/bulimics to describe themselves) through the giving of large quantities of milk, i.e. demand feeding. The second piece of advice from the wise person, the bringing back of the brother, emphasises the sibling pair as a step towards maturity instead of the parent/child. However, the story is not just a happy ever after story - the step-mother turns into a toad and still lurks around the castle steps. A reminder that our shadow self is still there.

This story used with either mixed groups or groups of eating disorder people, takes on all the dimensions of an epic myth. It is a story that seems to appeal to a wide variety of participants and lends itself ideally to dramatisation. Some stories stand for themselves and are not enhanced by being enacted. The *Laidley Worm* uncovers new insights and new levels of awareness, particularly when it is enacted through masks.

The following is an example of one way of working with this story with a mixed group of clients who attend various therapeutic groups in a hospital setting. There is a once-monthly all day dramatherapy group for people referred from their small, ongoing groups. The small groups provide the support structure for follow through after the intensive days. This group is used to working both with me and with dramatherapy. There are 15 people of ages ranging from 23 - 57 years.

Having told the group the skeleton outline of the story but not the end, I start with the first scene; when preparing material to use in this way, it is useful to 'block' the story into scenes (or units), either through the changes of location, or through the entry of major new characters. We can see from the above synopsis of the story that the first scene/unit is the family, when the prince/son decides to leave home, the second unit is when the queen/mother becomes ill and dies, and the third unit is when the princess/daughter looks after the king/father; the fourth unit is when the king/father is hunting in the forest and meets the woman/witch/step-mother and so on...

At my suggestion, everyone divides into small groups and takes the first unit - the family of four and spend a little time discussing this family, before choosing roles and working at a vignette of the son announcing that he is leaving home. All the group work at the same unit and we share the scenes. All of them have different themes - in one the son rushes in to an essentially quiet family and makes the announcement, and despite challenges from his two parents, he insists that he has got to see the world and goes. In another, the family is having a meal, and the son slowly gets round to the subject, and with difficulty says what he is going to do. A third presentation places the family in the context of a row between father and son, with the mother supporting her son against the father and the daughter silently agreeing with her mother. The result of the row is that the son decides to leave home. Another group start with a scene between the brother and sister, where the prince tells her of his plans, and asks her to support him when he tells the parents. The group present very short vignettes, and I then ask them to create a family sculpt of the dynamics of the family. All the sculpts reflect a division between mother and son and father and daughter. Notice that I am not yet moving into mask work.

I then ask the group to create three larger than life, exaggerated, physicalised (i.e. in the body - working from the guts outwards to the finger tips) sculpts of: mother becoming ill - mother dying - father and daughter left together, (encompassing units two and three). Sculpting in what I term a larger-than-life way, enables people to make transitions into character and to exaggerate all the expressions and feelings; sometimes I will push this to an epic sculpt (see Jennings, 1991), and people will stand on chairs, each other's shoulders, and find other ways to express the enormity of the character or scene. This is in complete contrast to miniature sculpting with objects and toys.

I then ask people to create masks, using a card-outline that they can draw round and colour how they wish. They create a mask for the daughter, father and the woman, and the groups enact the father leaving home, hunting in the forest, meeting the woman, asking her to marry him and sending messages back to the palace to make the preparation for the wedding. Then the whole group dramatise the arrival home, the wedding, and the person in the crowd that calls out that the princess is the most beautiful woman. The next unit is in fact the witch/step-mother preparing a spell to turn the princess into the worm, and I suggest that everyone uses the woman mask they have made, and creates her witch mask on the reverse side; in effect they now have a double sided mask of the woman who meets the king in the forest and the witch who creates the spell. Everybody in the group becomes the witch brewing spells either in groups or on their own, and the witch mask gives them a lot of freedom to invent the most potent brews and the most horrible outcomes.

I now suggest that people have some more time to create a mask for the worm and a mask for the wise person - I use the plain masks that can be cut, painted, and have things stuck on them for the worm. People suggest that the hair and beard is important for the wise-person (male stereotypes), so I have shredded computer paper available; one woman in the group says that she is an American Indian medicine woman - which enables the group to see that the wise person can be male or female or neither; the wise mask is to be made out of bits and pieces - material, cord, computer paper, wood-shavings, as well as paints of various sorts. (My rationale for this structure is that the worm-mask needs to be taken off easily therefore a mask base both contains it as well as facilitating the disengagement; the wise mask is intended to be integrated therefore it can be more expansive and creative).

(We have spent three hours so far - an hour on the early scenes - an hour on the forest and spell scenes and the drawing/painting of the card masks - then the final hour on the creation of the two masks). During the latter part, people have worked at their own pace, on their own or in small groups, asking for technical help if they need it, checking how masks look in mirrors. They are totally absorbed in the creation of these masks and have several relationships with them - the creator, then the struggle when the mask is not how they think it will be, testing the role when they put on the mask, and shaping and forming it.

Mask making itself is a therapeutic process and time needs to be given to the craft, in itself; people need to be told the time boundaries they have for the work.

When everyone has made their masks, I ask everyone to put on their worm masks and move round as the worm, and then to replace it with their wise mask, imagine themselves living up a mountain and looking down on the village scene, and to think to themselves what advice might be needed to help the village.

We then remove the masks and have a lunch break, making sure that the masks have been put safely in places where they will not be stepped or sat on.

Teaching point: I always work with the mask convention that they must be placed face-upwards. A mask placed face downwards means that the person is dead.

After the lunch break we re-assemble to work at the central scene (made up of several units) where the princess is discovered in her bed by her servants, having turned into the worm; she slithers out of the bed and goes to the sea shore, and coils herself round a rock; she starts to ravage the crops and countryside; the villagers go to the wise person for advice; they return and start to milk the cattle and feed the milk to the worm to keep it calm. Group members are invited to choose whether they want to be worm, wise persons or villagers/cattle; (it was interesting on this occasion that all the people who had been queen/mothers in the first and second units, chose to be cows in this scene). The group divides as follows:

> five people decide to be worm
> three people decide to be wise person
> four people decide to be cows
> three people decide to be villagers

(two of the cows agree to double up and play the servants also).

I suggest that the villagers and cows choose a simple prop to indicate who they are - the villagers choose hats and scarves from the prop box, and the cows spend some time giggling whether to create udders or horns - they decide to quickly draw the outline of a cow's face and horns and tie it on the top of their heads, so that when they are on their hands and knees it is then in the correct position. I give all the groups a few moments to discuss and try out their roles; the worms decide that they want a large sheet to cover them so that they look like one enormous monster.

Teaching point: Once a group has become engaged in a theme, it is possible for the group members to move in and out of role/character - try things out - change them. This gives them some autonomy and enables them to develop flexibility.

I suggest to the group that we work with the scenes from the worm being discovered to the point where she is being calmed with the milk. The group sets up the room for the scenes by using chairs covered with prop-box material to represent the village and country side in the centre space; at one end of the room the wise people place chairs on top of a large table for the mountain; and at the other end, the worm is concealed under a large sheet. One of the people decides to leave off her mask at the beginning so that she can appear asleep when her father comes in to say good-night to her. She then puts on her mask, the two servants come in and switch on a light and bid the princess good morning; they pull back the sheet and the worm starts to writhe; the servants scream and run away and the worm slithers towards the sea shore and curls up.

The villagers appear very curious and talk to each other; the worm then raises all its heads and starts to devour the countryside; the villagers are terrified and dare not go near it; they have a meeting and decide to go up to the mountain to consult with the wise person.

Teaching point: It is important for the dramatherapist to continue to structure and side-coach; i.e. to assist the transition from scene to scene and also to encourage and stimulate participants.

When the villagers reacted in fear to the worm, I said to them, 'What do the villagers decide to do now?' (side-coach). When they replied that they wanted a meeting, I turned to the worm and suggested that this was another scene and that they would be resting now (structure).

The villagers set off on a long walk and climb towards the mountain; they decide to sing as they walk, and one patient suggests that they sing 'Onward Christian Soldiers'. This leads to various marching songs until they reach the foot of the mountain. The villagers lie on the floor and pull themselves along, as if it is a cliff face, (they had remembered a mountain climbing project we had done in an earlier workshop); they climb on to the table and say to the wise people:

> We have come from the village and we need your advice.

The wise people respond in a chorus:

> We have seen your sorrow - what do you want?

Villagers:

> The worm is destroying everything; our crops, the hedges and trees; we are scared it will be our children next.

The wise people, individually:

> The worm is not vicious but frightened.
>
> She needs looking after; and calming.
>
> Choose your best cows, milk them and give her the milk; as much as she wants.

Then in chorus:

> But remember; she will only be well when her brother comes home again; that is all.

The villagers return down the mountain, and I side-coach, suggesting that they tell all the villagers what the wise people have said, so that they can all hear the wise words.

This they do, and then organise their cows, milk them and imagine they are carrying huge pails of milk on yokes to the worm. The worm meanwhile is devouring everything in sight; slowly as the many heads start to drink the milk, the worm begins to calm down; the villagers remember that the wise people have said she must have as much as she wants so they milk the cows twice and continue to pour huge pails to the worm. The worm eventually falls asleep, full to the brim of the milk.

I suggest we remove our masks and de-role from the characters and decide what we shall do next. The wise people come down off their mountain, the worm comes out from the sheet and the cows, worm and wise people all remove their masks. I ask how they felt it went, and they all take some time to surface; even the cows have stopped giggling. The worms all say they are very tired from all the writhing over the floor; and they feel very full (!). I suggest a few moments' break, for a stretch, loo, cigarette and so on. We re-assemble and discuss the next part of the story.

The group want to do the return of the brother and they suggest that he returns on a ship with his fellow sailors. I tell them that the boat is made from rowan which means it cannot be destroyed, even though the step-mother/witch sends a storm. The brother approaches the worm with raised sword to kill it, then hears his sister's voice asking to be kissed. The brother then waves a rowan branch over the step-mother who then turns into the toad.

The group set up the table as the ship and the people who had played brother before decide they are all on the ship. The rest of the group make the noise of the storm (side coach) and the worm wakes up and makes horrible sounds. The brothers come through the storm and leap onto the shore and all approach with uplifted swords; the princesses' voices all say:

'Don't kill me; kiss me, I am your sister.'

The brothers approach in some fear, kiss the worm, who removes the mask and becomes the princess again. The brother give them big hugs. (I side coach and say, 'And the witch?'); the brothers go to step mothers and wave the rowan branch, and she shrinks to a toad, and hisses horribly. The princesses place their worm masks on the step-mothers. The group say that they want to do a dance to finish and celebrate. They all remove their masks, hold hands and stamp and skip in a circle.

To close this session, I suggest we all sit in a circle and bring with us the wise mask we made. We have some feed-back through the character eg. 'When I was the princess I felt...' or 'As the work it was...'. Members of the group had a lot of satisfaction from enacting the story and their comments were very insightful.

'The milk is important for the worm.'
'Especially when it is as much as it wants.'
'The toad is always there.'
'I really felt I could be a wise person.'

and so on.

I suggest to the group that they all consider what the princess does now - and they can ask the wise mask they had made, for suggestions if they need to. They discuss this with the person sitting next to them for a few moments and then bring it back to the whole group.

Most people are of the opinion that the princess should go on a journey now - like her brother, she could now leave home; some people wonder what has happened to the king; one person says he is dead and the prince will now rule.

Figure 9 - Sad and angry masks using template

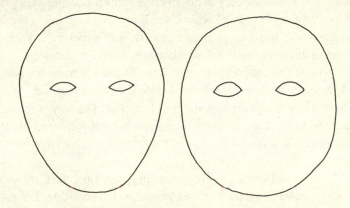

Figure 10 - Template shapes

Figure 11 - Mask 'diary' kept weekly using template mask

I ask them what the wise mask has to say and the following are some of the answers:

> 'I can be wise and not just a little girl'; 'I can remind you to take care of yourself'; 'Don't forget the mountain'; 'Don't forget the toad'; 'Find yourself a rowan branch.'

We spent the first half of the afternoon time on the dramatisation of the story and the second half on distancing from the masks, feeding-back as the character and then sharing any reflections about the day as a whole. This latter process took over an hour for people to feel sufficiently grounded to walk away from the experience.

Intensive dramatherapy groups of this kind are not currently used very frequently in therapeutic settings.[3] The majority of dramatherapists work in a weekly mode of groups lasting an hour and a half, a practice adopted from psychotherapy practice. Dramatherapy is still in its infancy in discovering appropriate forms for practice and relies heavily on the experience of other disciplines. One function of the laboratory research group at the Institute of Dramatherapy is to experiment with new time structures and to discover variations in relation to effective practice.

We have seen in this chapter how masks can be used in many varying forms in dramatherapy, both in direct work with peoples' life situations, and in more dramatically distanced ways through mythic characters. The way of the mask is rich and infinite,[4] and brings together both an art form in itself and a therapeutic journey for therapist and client alike.

> 'In its supportive, complementary function, the mask should make a character or idea immediately accessible. The potential weakness of the mask is that dramatists may use it in simplistic, reductive, confusing, or awkward ways.'
>
> *Harris Smith: Masks in Modern Drama, p 181*

Chapter Seven

The Dramatherapist: a frontiersperson waiting at the threshold

'Don't you feel brave to be going to the jungle?'
'Brave? When a journey has to be made, it has to be made;
I'm just a journeyperson.'

fragment of conversation en route to Malaysia

'...we might make a detailed examination of what is meant
by the immensity of the forest. For this "immensity" origin-
ates in a body of impressions, which,in reality, have little
connection with geographical information. We do not have
to be long in the woods to experience the always rather
anxious impression of "going deeper and deeper" into a
limitless world.'

Bachelard: The Poetics of Space, p 185

The writing of this book represents both a personal and professional journey on
which I have continued to explore the nature (and culture) of dramatherapy - its
philosophy, theory and practical application. It is also an attempt to communicate
the various processes that have happened to me that have interacted with my
scenarios and the many issues that exist on my stages as well as waiting in the wings.
    As Cox and Theilgaard say:

'...the therapist's life-story also comes within the ambit of
"the greater story". The life-stories of both patient and therapist are inevitably linked in a more profound way than
technical terms may suggest. Thus, phrases like "counter-
transference phenomenon" and "transient projective identi-
faction", technically necessary though they may be, may

shield a therapist from discerning a dimension of mutual predicament it is unwise to ignore.'

Cox and Theilgaard: Mutative Metaphors in Psychotherapy, p 8

I have become increasingly aware of the needs of dramatherapists themselves if they are to be these 'frontierspeople' waiting at the threshold of human experience on the stage of life. Because the dramatherapist is both actively and interactively engaged within the therapeutic drama, it places enormous demands on all their resources - resources that need constant replenishment and nourishment. As creative artist *and* therapist, these demands are doubly made. There are times of creative darkness as well as therapeutic impasse and professional disillusionment that can result in easy resort to institutionalisation of one's work, and of becoming prescriptive in practice. This is influenced by the additional demands of legitimising dramatherapy within the professional milieu and can result in attempts to define one's work by other practice - such as the suggestion that dramatherapy is a psychotherapy (see introduction). Another 'coping mechanism' is to become a technician in dramatherapy where the technique has precedence over the process.

Dramatherapists need to remind themselves constantly that they are first and foremost creative artists within the theatre and drama art forms which includes actor, director, scenic designer and writer and that the art form is a constant renewal of creativity for the therapist as well as the client.

It is not enough for drama workshops and theatre visits to cease at the end of training - when a course of training is complete is when the real task of the creative artist begins. The green actor newly out of drama school will be venturing timidly into developing a range of roles and personal style that continue to develop. Regular workshops, theatre going and exploration of text should form part of the continuing experience - and not only for the professional side of the dramatherapist; it is also important to feed the artist within, in its own right. The dramatherapist is not only placing his or her art at the service of therapy, but continuing to develop themselves artistically and creatively because that is their survival need - an artist is an artist because they *have* to be, and it is this pull to continue the unknown journey that is characteristic of the dramatherapist. If it were not so, I would have chosen to do something far less complex and demanding.

Part of my time is spent in providing resources for overseas training and developing staff groups, enabling them to discover or renew their own creative potential. The following example is from a staff training group which took place over one week. The group consisted of clinicians - psychologists, psychiatrists, nurses and occupational therapists who had little experience of drama and theatre but were high risk-takers in terms of their imagination. I chose for this course

Midsummer Night's Dream as a structure and in particular I wanted to explore a journey through the forest.

The forest is a powerful symbol for therapeutic journeys; forests contain mysteries, darkness, hiding places, shadows, creatures... Forests are places of encounter and change.

During the first day of the course we explored various images of the forest - the colours and textures, the environmental features - through movement and sound. We then explored the different creatures that inhabited the forest. Each person chose a forest creature that they wished to develop as their own character and several groups emerged -

> creatures of the earth
> > on the earth,
> > of the air,
> > of air and water.

Each creature had individual characteristics but also felt they had connections with their group. Individuals worked on their creature masks, using plaster bandage[1] and a costume constructed from material scraps, old tights and pieces of old sheeting. This process took place over two days as the creature characters slowly developed.

The third day we concentrated on the forest itself where these creatures lived and the group constructed an entire forest which contained their own particular environment - a river, waterfall, tall trees, hollow tree trunks, piles of leaves.

On the fourth day we looked at families who lived outside the forest and who might run away to the forest if home life became unacceptable. We set up several families where there were rigid parents that led children to run away. Having set up and shared the typical domestic scenes, we then explored the running away to the forest - half the group as the forest people and half as the run-aways and pursuers, and looked at changes and transformation that happened in the forest.

We then returned to the forest creatures themselves and gave them time to explore their forest and then write about themselves in role as forest creatures. The following is what they wrote:

The earth creatures

We are all new arrivals and each of us has come from another element. The 'wild pig' from the savannah, where there was plenty of light and space and where it lived an untroubled existence. It was attracted here by the food and the security. The 'parasitic creature' (sucker) came here from the life of a butterfly which lived in a meadow. The butterfly chose this place because of the security it offers. The 'chameleon' came here from the water and the life of a jelly-fish. It could see the possibilities of also becoming a land-animal in peace and quiet, and free from the necessity of having to move so often.

The three animals stay together in the forest because of the food under the branches, because other creatures come to their place in the forest, because there is water and because the course of the river changes naturally. Their place in the forest in central. It is secure and good and the plentiful food supply tames all their aggressive instincts.

The creatures who come from the earth

In the beginning, we were the earth. One day a creature appeared out of the earth - a gigantic creature, dark, heavy and slow, alone and powerful. Instincts such as inquisitiveness, aggression and wildness forced two new creatures to detach themselves. Their speed and range is different, as is their relationship to light.

The creatures from the water and the air

We have come from the water and we have been living in the water for thousands of years until we suddenly discovered that we were able to fly.

The old one arrived first in this place and chose it on account of the palm. He sleeps safely on the earth under the leaves of the magic tree. He eats the fishes - there are plenty of fishes in the water. He can fly up from the waterfall to fly high up against the sky.

The young one came here not so many thousand years ago. He moves still very much between the air and the water. He feels safe under the waterfall, where the water has a very airy form.

The creatures from the air

We give to the wood quietness and openness, but it is difficult when there is fighting in the wood.

We like to invite people to come into the wood, but on the condition that they are not allowed to destroy anything. If they do so, we will try to cast them out, but that can be difficult for one of us.

In the beginning, there was the magic forest, in which the trees, the mountains and the air were magic. From the magic mountain arises the fire-creature, from the magic tree arises the brain-creature, and from the magic air arises the spirit-creature.

We move around in the magic forest. We gel and strengthen from our magic origin. In our area of the forest there is a special kind of magic element. We can live for a long time in this area, and when we touch our magic element we become second-sighted. But if we were blind, magic power and second sight would be too much, and remembrance would destroy us.

On the final day, it was important to distance from the week's experience, to dismantle the forest and be able to stand outside the forest and its creatures and look in. We took down the forest, de-roled from the masks and costumes, shared 'as ourselves' and read through the diary we had kept throughout the week, (morning, mid-day and afternoon). There was still a struggle to distance from the forest and group members were unable to feel connected to their everyday selves and the work setting to which they would shortly be returning. It is crucial when exploring 'forest journeys' that people are able to come out of the forest and stay out - even if they choose to re-enter later on.

I brought in a small coffee table from the corridor and asked the group to re-construct the forest as a theatrical model that a designer might use, (the actual reverse of a play production). Twelve people with pipe cleaners, plaster and paint became totally absorbed in creating this replica of the forest in miniature. They were meticulous about detail and wanted every feature re-created. I then asked them to make a two inch model of their forest creature and place it in the forest - again, complete absorption and an ensuing delight at what they had created.

What was happening was that people were literally able to stand outside the experience and look in and grasp it in its totality. As Wilshire says:

> 'Theatre with its fictions so organizes and compresses, or reduces, expands, or speeds up the presentation of events, that it can bring the whole - say a whole action within the world - before the mind; thus it allows it to be taken in as a whole.'

> *Wilshire: Role Playing and Identity, p 33*

The enormity of the week's experience needed some reduction to make it manageable so that we could walk away from it - we find this often in the use of sculpting and small personal re-constructions of life events, (see also Jennings and Minde, 1990).[2]

The group had not made the connection with *A Midsummer Night's Dream* until I shared it with them on the day before - one group member had brought in the text in her own language and we read Puck's closing speech in both languages as a way of closing:

> 'If we shadows have offended,
> Think but this, and all is mended:

That you have but slumbered here
While these visions did appear'

Shakespeare: A Midsummer Night's Dream, V.i

I am writing elsewhere on the dramatherapeutic structure of *A Midsummer Night's Dream* - but its basic theme may be summarised as:

Rigid families - journey through the forest - encounter with pain and chaos - transformation and reconciliation.

This is a very useful metaphor for a therapeutic journey and one which moves through constant and recurring moon symbolism and imagery of fertility, an interaction between class structures (upper/lower classes) and between worlds (human/spirit world). It is one of the workmen who says (rather like the prisoners I work with):

'I have had a most rare vision'

Shakespeare: A Midsummer Night's Dream, IV. i

Another example of the use of dramatherapy as a staff resource is shown in a seminar I was asked to run for people working in child abuse. I suggested that the seminar should be a resource for professional people, not just a session on techniques.

I started with a picture of Perseus, Pegasus, Andromache and the sea monster, but did not tell the group the source - some thought it was *St George and the Dragon*.

I asked the group to colour the picture for themselves - people remarked as they coloured that it was like play-school and some people entered into the spirit of it; others seemed a little uneasy - one person seemed hostile and tense.

There were many variations in how the picture was perceived - some people thought the knight had wings, others thought the woman pregnant, some thought the dragon had already been wounded and coloured the sea red with blood and others thought the knight had arrived just in time.

The tense person said:

'I have got to appear in court next week - I need some help'.

I asked him who was on trial and he said:

'Fathers, I mean the father - for sexual abuse of a teenage daughter - she calls him a monster'.

I said to him and all the group, 'if the monster is on trial, who is judging?' He was speechless - some of the group said the knight or the woman; others disagreed saying they could not judge because they were involved - then someone else said 'the sea'-

Perseus and Andromache

'The sea knows all - it's been there since the beginning'.

A ripple went round the group at the idea of the sea as judge -

Therapist: What other words do we have for judge?

Critic - controller - no, he's impartial - always *he*, said one member - he/she watches and listens - and waits - weighs up both sides - directs - condemns -

Therapist: Let's form two groups - those who are in touch with
                    judgement, control and punishment in one group and those
                    who are watching, listening and impartial in the second group.

The group splits unevenly - seven people go to judgement (Group 1) and five people to watching (Group 2). Three out of the four men go to Group 1.

Therapist: Remember about the image of the sea as possibly the judge
                    of the monster. Write down as a group all the judge/sea
                    words that come to mind; do it quickly, without thinking.

I gave them six minutes to free-associate and then to create a sculpt from those words, together with sound.

Group One's words		Group Two's words	
Deep	Controlling	Waiting	Ripples
Drowning	Albatross	Still	Waves
Death	Shipwreck	Deep	Containing
Punishment	Curse	Watching	Movement
Hell	Pirate	Turbulent	Change
Overpowering	Keel-hauling	Ancient	Patience
Fathoms			

Group One's sculpt had a central figure kneeling with another swathed round its neck as an albatross, two people as an enormous wave overpowering them, two people with hands joined on either side of the kneeling figure pulling one way and the other, and one person looking on with a finger raised as though giving a pronouncement.

Group Two's sculpt used three people joining hands in a circle, moving near the ground in a circle, moving near the ground and slowly moving in ripples upwards to standing, becoming tempestuous and calming again; one person sitting cross-legged in the middle, waiting and another outside, looking in with arms held open and outstretched.

The participants remarked on the similarities between the sculpts and the man awaiting the court appearance said that he felt like the person with the albatross round his neck. He then asked if he could enact the court scene he would appear in. I suggested that we finished with the sea-images and the picture and then consider his own situation.

He then said that he would like to be Pegasus and fly, whereupon someone else said, 'but you'll still have St George on your back.'

Therapist: I suggest that we make groups of the different
                          elements of the picture - knight, monster, woman, horse
                          and sea.

The group moved around and divided in the following way:

Knight: 3 people (2 male 1 female)

Monster: 3 people (1 male 2 female)

Woman: no one

Horse: 2 people (1 male 1 female)

Sea: 4 people (4 female)

I asked them to create the picture using groups instead of individuals. I then asked each group to write about themselves as a character, and also what they wanted to say to the others.

This is a transcript of what they wrote:

SEA

I am sea
I am constant but ever changing
I am powerful and strong
I will be there when woman, knight and monster have gone
I am three dimensional
I have depths which cannot be seen
I can change from my pathway, but continue
I can fit into many shapes and places
I am neither good nor evil

To the woman

You are uncaring
You are not watching the knight or the serpent
You are static; like a statue
You are cold and calculating
You are a strong minded woman

To the serpent:

You are frightening to look at
You cannot help the way you look
You are a victim of circumstance
You are in conflict
You are afraid
You will terrorise because you must survive

To the Pegasus

You are an innocent party
You are blinkered and cannot see which way you are going
You are goodness
You are magical, with wings
You have grace and lightness

To the knight

You do not reveal your feelings
You have control of the scythe and horse
You are powerful
You are aggressive

PEGASUS

I am Pegasus
I am gentle
I am strong
I can fly

To the knight

This person that rides me has stolen me
He has covered my face and harnessed me

I am forced to take part in this battle as he dictates
My rider is cruel and will not let me leave his spurs that cut my flesh
I am forced to watch the destruction of this monster that may not have
  committed any harm

To the woman

You are pregnant
You are powerful
You have the power to stop this battle
You are smug
You are self-satisfied
You are reticent in using your power to
  call a halt - you are cruel

To the monster

You are ugly
You are friendly
You have sharp teeth
You like biscuits
You are like a friendly dog - sometimes
  you are naughty and chew the wrong thing

To the sea

You will be here when this scene is gone
You are home to many
You are feared by some
You are a friend to some
You are a home to this monster
You can be a tempest
You can be calm

KNIGHT

I am the Protector
I am swift, strong, not just physical
I am bright, decisive, angry, anonymous
I am triumphant

To the woman

You are frozen, you are mine
You are pathetic, you are passionate
You are assertive and directive
You are in need of help
You are confused and angry

To the monster

You are evil and out of control
You are in pain, sick and in need of help
You are destructive and powerful and use your energy misdirectedly

MONSTER

I am angry
I am helpless and powerless
I am innocent and naive
I am a victim
I am being drowned in my own surroundings
I am being annihilated
I am misinterpreted and misunderstood
I am exploited and suppressed
I am protesting

To the woman

You are manipulative
You are in control
You are deceptive and seductive
You are exploited and exploiting
You are silent and scheming
You are abusing your power as a woman
You are pure yet all knowing
You are innocent and wise
You are guilty
You are in command of the situation
You are crushed

To the knight

You are blindly violent
You are powerful
You are assuming
You are dangerous and ignorant
You are crushing
You are being used
You are exploited
You are misunderstanding the situation
You are angry and unsympathetic
You are blundering
You are afraid of consequences

To the sea

You are wild
You are engulfing
You are supportive
You are neutral
You are independent
You are on-looking
You are constant
You are confused
You are nurturing (restorative)
You are dangerous and threatening
You are benign

To Pegasus

You are used and abused
You are exploited
You are innocent
You are a victim
You are a slave to man
You are a war machine
You are benign and good
You are manipulated
You are afraid for own safety

The group used these words as a chorus to each other.

The man who wanted the court scene said that, as Pegasus, he realised he was burdened with the 'saviour image' and needed to get into the sea and float for a while.

The importance of this session was to discover that it was possible not to fall into the trap of explaining and giving answers. The group as a whole and all the individuals within it felt that they had been through a profound experience with multiple themes and perceptions, as well as surprising themselves with their own creativity. Their creative journey had taken them through embodiment, projection and role. Their journey took them into realms they had not dreamt of and gave them experiences of life not yet lived.

It is important for me to include something about my own travel and travail as I near the ending of this book. I do not want this to be an end, but a pause as I rest on a plateau and survey a backward view of my own life and also the journey that the book itself has taken.

The journey of this book has involved many special people - clients, colleagues, trainees and friends on their various pathways, as well as my own personal and professional highways and low ways; my own journey is at times alone, and at times peopled by people mingling their images, dreams and dramas with my own.

There have been moments of immensity which have reduced me to silence, and at other times it has been an effort to traverse a toadstool.[4]

I have been silenced by the *Mahabharata*, particularly after seeing the breath-stopping production by Peter Brook (my diary at the time reads, 'I am transported, helpless and feel very, very small; I could move mountains...'), and the following quotation comes to mind:

> 'Death has entered the heart of kings. We must now expect suffering, madness. You, ponder deeply, don't be afraid of your dreams and watch over the earth'.
>
> *Mahabharata, p 54.*

and I can feel like James the snail in A. A. Milne's *The Four Friends*, who:

> 'went a journey with the goat's new compass and he reached the end of his brick'.
>
> *Milne: When We Were Very Young, p 11*

The theatre makes it more possible to experience the epic and the micro - to move between immensity and miniature:

'Now the hungry lion roars'.
'Not a mouse
Shall disturb this hallowed house.'

Shakespeare: A Midsummer Night's Dream, V.i

and

'There is a special providence in the fall of a sparrow.'

Shakespeare: Hamlet, V.ii

Such experiences continue to be both devastating and humbling.

The theatre contains both the chaos and the drama to order it, so that it may be revisited yet again - the moving image cannot stay the same. And yet all of your dramas connect you to my dramas; we come together in the theatre of life - or in the life of the theatre.

'Immensity is within ourselves. It is attached to a sort of expansion of being that life curbs and caution arrests, but which starts again when we are alone'.

Bachelard: The Poetics of Space, p 184

'I have hands to pluck you,
wee thyme of my dreams,
rosemary of my excessive palor'.

Andre Breton, quoted in Bachelard, op.cit.

The theatre continues to be a place of healing with the drama of being. The theatre is the means of transformation. After half a century of journeying, it has just begun and my cobwebbed eyes are only beginning to open.[5]

'ARJUNA: Vyasa, do you know the end of your poem?
VYASA: I'm not sure it has an end.
ARJUNA: Are you sure, at least, if death catches up with us
all, that someone someday will survive?
VYASA: Yes, I am sure. I even have the proof: this child who
accompanies me and questions me, and to whom I relate
the chaos of the past.'

Mahabharata, p 55

Never lose the passion that moves mountains and that mountains move, that can journey in the dark and rest in the light. The child and the old person come together in fortitude, while they glimpse yet again the chasm and the gazelle.

Notes on Chapters

Introduction

1. Of course this list could continue to include non-theatre literature; novels, poems. It is a given that dramatherapists are conversant with the Old and New Testament and other great religious writings; have a storehouse of myths and fairy stories; and continually participate in their own theatre art form.

2. A number of dramatherapists have a leaning towards Jung in terms of symbolic understanding; however, there is a vast range of material from many different writers which does not necessarily need to be exclusive. *Day of Shining Red*, Lewis, 1978 is an important book on symbol, metaphor and ritual.

3. A good introduction to psychodrama is *Acting In* by Adam Blatner. There are many good books now available, which make easier reading than Moreno's own originals.

4. The British Association for Dramatherapists has approved all five dramatherapy training programmes in the UK for their full membership: The Institute of Dramatherapy, London; Sesame at Central School of Speech and Drama, London; St Johns College, York; Hertfordshire College, St Albans; and South Devon College, Torquay, as well as the course run by the Hellenic Society for Theatre and Therapy, Greece.

Chapter One

1. Many theories of play focus on a *function* such as social play or cognitive play; two very imaginative books which focus on process are: Oaklander,*Windows to our Children*, 1978 and Bloch, *So the Witch Won't Eat Me*, 1978. For a detailed theory and practice see Jennings, *Symbolic Play in Therapy*, in preparation, Blackwell Scientific.

2. See for example *Romeo and Juliet*; the Nurse in I.iii illustrates superbly 're-working' past experience.

3. 'if the dream is psychic nature per se, unconditioned, spontaneous, primary, and this psychic nature can show a dramatic structure, then the nature of the mind is poetic.' See Hillman, *Healing Fiction* 1983, pp 35-40 for a brilliant development of Jung's ideas on the dramatic nature of dreams. I was not aware, when writing, of this particular book of Hillman's which is essential reading for dramatherapists.

4. Domhoff, *The Mystique of Dreams*, 1985 shows how a western culture can project onto an alternative culture a romantic yearning of how they wish themselves to be; some readers will be aware of an approach to dream therapy based on this kind of projection.

5. 'Only when a narrative receives inner coherence in terms of the depths of human nature do we have fiction, and for this fiction we have to have plot...To plot is to move from asking the question "and then what happened?" to the question "why did it happen?" In our kind of fictions the plots are our theories.' Hillman op.cit.

8. *Shakespeare: The Play Within*, is the working title of my research at the Shakespeare Institute which will form the basis of a future book for dramatherapists.

Chapter Two

1. See, for example, Foulkes, *Introduction to Group-Analytic Psychotherapy*, 1948 reprinted 1983, or Lear, ed., *Spheres of Group Analysis*, undated. Psychotherapy has many theories and models which are currently being made more explicit through the intention to get one psychotherapy umbrella for EEC entry in 1992. Art, Music and Drama Therapy are proposing a Creative Arts Therapy section.

2. Look at the work of Stanislavski, Meyerhold, Halprin, and Brook, described in Roose-Evans, *Experimental Theatre from Stanislavski to Peter Brook.* Dramatherapists have often found that there is a general sense of improved well-being when patients develop the physical means of expressing themselves through a drama-movement programme.

3. Van der Post's books are an important resource for dramatherapists, especially *The Lost World of the Kalahari* and *The Heart of the Hunter*; see pp 132-134 for the story of the lady from the stars. Gersie and King, *Storymaking in Education and Therapy*, 1990, is an excellent book for practitioners.

Chapter Three

1. The Temiar make use of the river as a spatial metaphor to organise their concepts of people in space. The river also has an important physical reality to them as being a safe form of journeying, and a danger-free source of food.

2. I cannot stress enough the importance of dramatherapists being conversant with the aims and effects of medication and having regular consultation with the medical practitioners, including GPs.

3. Dr Shmuel Lahad has developed a statistically viable method of assessment through the use of story making described in *Community Stress Prevention*, 1988 and elaborated in Jennings, *Dramatherapy Theory and Practice Vol. II*, 1990 . Kelly's Repertory Grid is also invaluable for dramatherapists. It is described in Bannister and Fransella, *Inquiring Man*, 1986 and its detailed application in dramatherapy practice in Grainger, *Drama and Healing*, 1990.

Chapter Four

1. There are many basic drama books with excellent structures for improvisation; however, consider Hornbrook, *Education and Dramatic Arts*, 1989, as an important caution concerning the loss of the theatre art form in many drama approaches. Spolin, *Improvisation for the Theatre*, 1973, Johnstone op.cit. and Barker, *Theatre Games*, 1977, for good working ideas.

2. Old photographs, postcards of people and places, all make useful starting points for the drama work. Sometimes I have used just a single image; at other times I have a selection of pictures for individuals, families or groups to make choices. Some pictures follow a theme, e.g. different kinds of doors, different family groupings.

3. The dramatherapist's function is increasingly developing elements of theatre direction in the ensuing scenes. Perhaps after the democratic '60s, we are all scared of using the word 'director' and associate it with taking control! However, at one level the dramatherapist has to be in control on behalf of the clients.

4. In groups where writing is difficult for participants, people can speak their character analysis and, if desired, the therapist can write it down.

5. Working in the integrated model (see pages 39-46) of dramatherapy is most useful for families, often in conjunction with other forms of therapy. Also with couples who attend groups - I use this way of working with people suffering from problems concerning their fertility.

Chapter Five

1. Landy has practiced and written extensively on one-to-one dramatherapy, in *Dramatherapy Concepts and Practice*, 1986 and 'One-on-One' in Jennings ed. 1991 op.cit. Landy is both an actor and theatre director as well as a dramatherapist.

2. Many people who ritually starve themselves talk about being heavy, as if the psychological burdens can be removed through the loss of weight.

3. For an elaboration of a diagnostic programme with adolescents see Jennings and Gersie, 'Dramatherapy with Disturbed Adolescents' in Jennings 1987 op.cit. A thinking through of dramatherapy with adolescents appears in *The Special Educational Needs Review*, ed. Jones, 1989 in the chapter 'The Trying Time' of which the example of Eddie is an extract.

Chapter Six

1. As Hornbrook op.cit. so clearly states, 'The model of a dramatised society is the backdrop to dramatic art. In it, we are described not simply as role-playing individuals acting out our preferences against a known "objective" world, but rather as moral agents making

sense of ourselves and our actions through our membership of communities of discourse.'

2. If someone says, 'I have not got a mask - I am nothing - I am a blank...' suggest they create a mask of a blank person, a nothing person and so on. Similarly if someone says, 'I can't remember something', ask them to make it up, (e.g. a dream, a family incident).

3. As groups become more confident, they are also able to side coach within the dramatic mode. Another approach to an intensive group of this kind is to set up a dramatic scenario and say to people, 'you are all a character in this scene', (e.g. a wedding, funeral).

4. An important summary of many approaches to mask work is Harris Smith, *Masks in Modern Drama*, 1984.

Chapter Seven

1. Plaster of Paris bandage is a means to create masks directly on peoples' faces, when they have their eyes protected and a covering of Vaseline on their skin. It is a method that needs a lot of practice before using it with clients and there can be problems with skin allergy and eye irritation.

2. In *Art Therapy and Dramatherapy: their relation and practice*, 1990, Ase Minde and I describe how we used the reducing of material to allow people to de-role; the scene in question was when people had painted large, frozen and bleak landscapes; before ending the group, they painted a small 'photograph' of their picture which they could put in their pocket.

3. *Shakespeare: The Play Within*, op.cit.

4. 'If there were no eternal consciousness in a man, if at the bottom of everything there were only a wild ferment, a power that twisting in dark passions produced everything great or inconsequential; if an unfathomable, insatiable emptiness lay hid beneath everything, what would life be then but despair?' Kierkegaard, *Fear and Trembling*: trans. Hannay 1985, Penguin.

5. 'the eye of man hath not heard, the ear of man hath not seen, man's hand is not able to taste, his tongue to conceive, nor his heart to report what my dream was!' Bottom in *A Midsummer Night's Dream*.

Bibliography

References cited in the text

Bachelard, G., 1968, *The Poetics of Space*, trans. Jolas, Beacon Press, Boston.

Bannister, D., and Fransella, F., 1986, *Inquiring Man*, Croom Helm, London

Barker, C., *Theatre Games*, Methuen, London

Blatner, H. A., 1973, *Acting In*, Springer, New York.

Bloch, D., 1978, *'So the Witch Won't Eat Me'*, Grove Press inc, New York.

Boal, A., 1974, *Theatre of the Oppressed*, Pluto Press, London

Brook, P., 1972, *The Empty Space*, Penguin, London.

Brook, P., 1988, *The Shifting Point*, Methuen, London

Cox, M., and Theilgaard, A., 1987, *Mutative Metaphors in Psychotherapy*, Tavistock, London.

Domhoff, G.,W., 1985, *The Mystique of Dreams*, University of California Press, Berkeley.

Foulkes, S. H., 1948, *Introduction to Group-analytic Psychotherapy*, Maresfield Reprints, London.

Gersie, A., and King, N., 1990, *Storymaking in Education and Therapy*, Jessica Kingsley, London.

Grainger, R., 1988-89, Drama Therapy and Thought Disorder, unpublished papers
1990, *Drama and Healing: the Roots of Drama Therapy*, Jessica Kingsley, London.

Harris Smith, S., 1984, *Masks in Modern Drama*, University of California Press, London, Berkeley.

Hillman, J., 1983, *The Healing Fiction*, Station Hill, New York.

Hornbrook, D., 1989, *Education and Dramatic Art*, Blackwell Educational, Oxford.

Huizinga, J., 1955, *Homo Ludens: A Study of the Play Element in Culture*, Beacon Press, Boston.

Jennings, S., 1973, *Remedial Drama*, A & C Black, London.

Jennings, S., 1973, 'The Kuda Kepang: Javanese Hobby Horse in Malaysia.' Dissertation. LSE.

Jennings, S., 1975, ed., *Creative Therapy*, Kemble Press, Banbury.

Jennings, S., 1978, 'Dramatherapy: the Anomalous Profession', *J Dramatherapy*, Vol. 1, no. 4

Jennings, S., 1978, 'Beware of Drama', *J Speech and Drama*, Vol. 27, no. 3.

Jennings, S., 1984, 'Models of Practice in Dramatherapy', *J Dramatherapy*, Vol. 7, no. 1.

Jennings, S., 1985, 'Temiar Dance and the Maintenance of Order' in *Society and the Dance*, Spencer, P., ed., CUP, Cambridge.

Jennings, S., 1986, *Creative Drama in Groupwork*, Winslow Press, Bicester.

Jennings, S., 1987, ed., *Dramatherapy Theory and Practice*, Routledge, London.

Jennings, S., 1988, 'Rights and Rites? Innovation in the Teaching of Medical Students', *J Holistic Medicine*, Vol. 3.

Jennings, S., 1988, 'The Loneliness of the Long Distance Therapist', *Brit J Psychotherapy*, Vol. 4, no. 3.

Jennings, S., 1988, 'Shakespeare and Gossip', presented at Shakespeare and the Mind Symposium, London.

Jennings, S., 1989, 'Thoughts black...a sense of evil in a therapeutic setting', Keynote presentation at the Arts Therapies Conference, N.Israel.

Jennings, S., 1989, 'The Epic Metaphor: The Paradox of Dramatherapy', presented at the Group Analytic Society.

Jennings, S., 1989, 'You speak like a green girl...', presented at the first International Symposium on Dramatherapy and Shakespeare, Stratford.

Jennings, S., 1989, 'The Trying Time: Dramatherapy with Adolescents', in *Special Educational Needs Review*, ed. Jones, Falmer Press, London and New York.

Jennings, S., 1990 ii. with Ase Minde, *Art Therapy and Dramatherapy: Their Relation and Practice*, Jessica Kingsley, London.

Jennings, S., 1990 iii. Ed., *Dramatherapy Theory and Practice Vol. 2*, Routledge, London.

Jennings, S., 1990 iv. with Elizabeth Rees, *Christian Symbols, Ancient Roots*, Jessica Kingsley, London.

Jennings, S., 1991 (in preparation), *Symbolic Play in Therapy*, Blackwell Scientific, Oxford and London.

Jennings, S., 1991, *Drama Ritual and Transformation*, Routledge, London.

Jennings, S., and Gersie, A., 1987, 'Dramatherapy with Disturbed Adolescents', in Jennings, ed., op.cit.

James, H., 1984, *The Aspern Papers* , ed. Curtis, Penguin, London.

James, H., 1984,*Turn of the Screw*, ed. Curtis, Penguin, London.

Johnstone, K., 1981, *Impro: Improvisation for the Theatre*, Methuen, London.

Kierkegaard, S., 1985, *Fear and Trembling* (trans. Hannay), Penguin, London.

Lahad, S., ed., 1988, *Community Stress Prevention*, CSPC, Kiryat Shmona, Israel.

Lahad, S., 1990, 'Bibliotherapy as Means of Assessing Coping Skills', in Jennings, op. cit.

Landy, R., 1986, *Drama Therapy: Concepts and Practice*, Charles C. Thomas, Springfield.

Landy, R., 1990, 'One-on-One', in Jennings, op.cit.

Lear, T., ed., undated, *Spheres of Group Analysis*, Group Analytic Society.

Lewis, G., 1982, *The Day of Shining Red*, CUP, Cambridge.

Mead, G. H., 1934, *Mind, Self and Society* (ed. Morris), University of Chicago Press, Chicago.

Miles, B., and Trewin, J. C., 1981, *Curtain Calls*, Lutterworth Press, Guildford.

Milne, A. A., 1989 (new edition), *When We Were Very Young*, Methuen, London.

Neihardt, J. G., 1972, *Black Elk Speaks*, Lincoln, London.

Oaklander, V., 1978, *Windows to our Children*, Real People Press, Utah.

Piaget, J., 1962 (repr.), *Play Dreams and Imitation in Childhood*, RKP, London.

Plato, 1974, (trans. Lee), *The Republic*, Penguin, London.

Roose-Evans, J., 1984, *Experimental Theatre from Stanislavsky to Peter Brook*, Routledge, London.

Scheff, T. J., 1979, *Catharsis in Healing, Ritual and Drama*, University of California Press, Berkeley.

Spolin, V., 1973, *Improvisation for the Theatre*, Pitman, London.

Stanislavski, C., 1968, *Building a Character*, Methuen, London.

Turner, V., 1982, *From Ritual to Theatre*, Performing Arts Journal Publishing, New York City.

van der Post, L., 1965, *The Lost World of the Kalahari*, Penguin, London.
   The Heart of the Hunter, Penguin, London.

Willett, J., (trans. and ed.), 1964, *Brecht on Theatre*, Methuen, London.

Wilshire, B., 1982, *Role Playing and Identity*, Indiana University Press, Bloomington.

Winnicott, D. W., 1974, *Playing and Reality*, Penguin, London.

Play scripts quoted in the text

Bely, A., 1985, *The Jaws of the Night*, in *Doubles, Demons and Dreamers: an international collection of symbolist drama* (ed. Gerould), Performing Arts Journal Publications, New York.

Carriere, J. C., 1987, *The Mahabharata*, a play based on the Indian Classic Epic, (trans. Brook), Methuen, London.

Lorca, F. G., 1988, *Three Tragedies: Blood Wedding, Yerma, The House of Bernarda Alba*, (trans. Graham-Lujan/O'Connell), Penguin, London.

Pirandello, L., 1979, *Six Characters In Search of an Author* in *Three Plays* (trans. Rietty/Mitchell/Londstrom), Methuen, London.

Shakespeare: *Hamlet, A Midsummer Night's Dream, Henry V, As You like It, Romeo and Juliet, The Tempest*. New Penguin Editions.

Sophocles, *Antigone* in *Greek Drama*, ed. Hadas, 1965, Bantam Books, London.

Suggested further reading

Berry, C., 1973, *Voice and the Actor*, Harrap, London.

Cox, M., 1988, *Structuring the Therapeutic Process*, amended edition, Jessica Kingsley, London.

Cox, M., 1988, *Coding the Therapeutic Process*, amended edition, Jessica Kingsley, London.

Dunne, J. S., 1973, *Time and Myth*, SCM Press, London.

van den Berg, K. T., 1985, *Playhouse and Cosmos*, Associated University Press, London and NJ.

von Franz, 1977, *Individuation in Fairytales*, Spring Publications, Dallas.

Heilpern, J., 1977, *Conference of the Birds: the Story of Peter Brook in Africa*, Penguin, London.

Hobson, R. F., 1985, *Forms of Feeling*, Tavistock, London.

Kott, J., 1988, *Shakespeare Our Contemporary* (repr.), Routledge, London.

Kumiega, J., 1987, *The Theatre of Grotowski*, Methuen, London.

Jung, C., 1963, *Memories, Dreams and Reflections*, Collins, London.

O'Connor, G., 1989, *The Mahabharata: Peter Brook's Epic in the Making*, Hodder and Stoughton, London.

White, R. S., 1986, *Innocent Victims: Poetic Injustice in Shakespearean Tragedy*, The Athlone Press, London.

Williams, D., 1988, *Peter Brook - A Theatrical Casebook*, Methuen, London.

The Author

Sue Jennings spent her early life in the professional theatre as a dancer, actor and choreographer before developing her innovatory work in remedial drama and dramatherapy in special schools, hospitals and prisons. She has brought her many years' experience of theatre, individual and group psychotherapy together with her postgraduate studies in social and medical anthropology into a synthesis of dramatherapy practice and training. Her work has taken her to many countries where she has established dramatherapy initiatives, including Norway, Denmark, Greece and Israel. She spent two years in the Malaysian rain forest with her three children while studying the Temiar people; her doctoral thesis, 'Drama, Ritual and Transformation' is to be published by Routledge. She established the Remedial Drama Centre in the 1960s, Dramatherapy Consultants and the British Association for Dramatherapists in the 1970s, and in the 1980s founded the Institute of Dramatherapy. The Institute is based in a professional theatre called Onstage, in Chalk Farm, London, and provides both dramatherapy and playtherapy training as well as dramatherapy research and client resource. The most recent development is an actors' clinic and a consultancy service for the professional theatre for directors, actors and writers. Her work at the London Hospital Medical College provides dramatherapy and arts resources for people with fertility problems, as well as training for doctors and counsellors. Her dramatherapy practice includes work with eating disorders, victims of abuse, and more recently a developing specialism in forensic dramatherapy. She is spending an increasing amount of time in the professional theatre, both as an actor and also in academic research at the Shakespeare Institute, exploring the relationship between dramatherapy and Shakespeare. Her many publications include *Remedial Drama* (A & C Black, 1973), *Creative Therapy* (Kemble Press, 1975), *Creative Drama in Group Work* (Winslow Press, 1986) and *Dramatherapy Theory and Practice* (Routledge, 1987).

Professional Organisations

Association for Dance Movement Therapy
99 South Hill Park, London NW3 2SP

British Association for Art Therapists
11A Richmond Road, Brighton BN2 3RL

British Association for Dramatherapists
The Old Mill, Tolpuddle, Dorchester, Dorset DT2 7EX

British Association for Music Therapy
69 Avondale Avenue, East Barnet, Hertfordshire EN4 8NB

Dramatherapy Consultants
PO Box 32, Stratford upon Avon CV37 6GU

The Institute of Dramatherapy
37 Chalk Farm Road, London NW1 6RN
tel: (071) 267 9649

Index